VERGING
ON THE ABYSS

Recent titles in
Contributions in Women's Studies

VERGING ON THE ____
____ ABYSS

The Social Fiction of Kate Chopin and Edith Wharton

MARY E. PAPKE

Contributions in Women's Studies, Number 119

Greenwood Press

NEW YORK • WESTPORT, CONNECTICUT • LONDON

Library of Congress Cataloging-in-Publication Data

Papke, Mary E.
 Verging on the abyss : the social fiction of Kate Chopin and Edith
Wharton / Mary E. Papke.
   p.   cm. — (Contributions in women's studies, ISSN 0147–104X ;
no. 119)
 Includes Bibliographical references and index.
 ISBN 0–313–26877–0 (alk. paper)
 1. Chopin, Kate, 1851–1904—Political and social views.
2. Wharton, Edith, 1862–1937—Political and social views.
3. American fiction—Women authors—History and criticism.   4. Women
and literature—United States.   5. Social problems in literature.
I. Title. II. Series.
PS1294.C63Z85   1990
813'.409355—dc20   90-38412

British Library Cataloguing in Publication Data is available.

Library of Congress Catalog Card Number: 90-38412
ISBN: 0–313–26877–0
ISSN: 0147–104X

First published in 1990

Greenwood Press, 88 Post Road West, Westport, CT 06881
An imprint of Greenwood Publishing Group, Inc.

Printed in the United States of America

The paper used in this book complies with the
Permanent Paper Standard issued by the National
Information Standards Organization (Z39.48–1984).

10 9 8 7 6 5 4 3 2

In memory
of
Angus Papke Dunn

Contents

Acknowledgments

This book, because it has been a very long time in the making, has gone through numerous transformations and incurred many debts. I owe thanks to Donald Bouchard and Donald Theall of McGill University, who encouraged me early on in my doctoral studies to pursue my interest in feminist critical theory and practice; I offer my sincerest thanks to Michael Bristol for his assistance, patience, and guidance on my first extended reading of Chopin's and Wharton's social fiction.

I owe thanks as well to many friends and colleagues for their support and encouragement during that first stage of seemingly endless labor. Doris Bristol, Eileen Manion, Julia Visor, Margaret Foley, Carol Neely, and Kristina Straub kept me thinking about and questioning my own work. William Morgan, who during that period undertook another long-term feminist critical project with me, gave me insight into important but elusive differences between male and female sensibilities and sensitivities; Linda Brodkey's analysis of that particular dialogue served to sharpen my self-criticism. I am also grateful to members of the various contentious but always engaging critical reading groups in which I have participated in Montreal, Normal, and Knoxville for shared perceptions. I wish to acknowledge my deepest gratitude to my parents, who have given me courage, inspiration, and love without reserve; without their support, I would never have entered the second stage of my project.

My work would also have been impossible without the considerable assistance of the McGill University McLennan Library staff, particularly the librarians in the Interlibrary Loan Service. I thank as well the staffs of the Illinois State University Library and the University of Tennessee John C. Hodges Library who facilitated my continued research on women writers. I should like to thank several antiquarian booksellers who searched for Wharton first editions and then sold them to me at ridiculously low prices, but I shall keep their names to myself.

In addition, the English Department of the University of Tennessee enabled me to begin the considerable revision and expansion my first stage work required. I am grateful in particular for a John C. Hodges summer research grant awarded me in 1989 by the Better English Fund and for the opportunity I have been given to teach numerous courses in my area of specialization. I should also like to thank both Bernard Koloski who accepted my essay on Chopin's pre-*Awakening* stories for his collection entitled *Approaches to Teaching Chopin's* The Awakening as well as the Modern Language Association of America which gave me permission to reprint portions of that work here.

Finally, my greatest indebtedness is to my husband, Allen Dunn. While he has not had to suffer with me the entire gestation and intense labor this book occasioned, he was my coach during the worst part of it. In the face of my own manic behavior this last year and despite the many responsibilities weighing upon him, he has remained ever optimistic, supportive, and loving. There are simply no words which can express my thanks for what he has given me, but, then, that seems fitting, for it is he who has shown me the unspeakable delectation possible between men and women.

Introduction

Christa Wolf, a contemporary German novelist, writes, in *The Quest for Christa T.*:

Christa T. said she didn't like things to be fixed: that everything, once it's out there in existence—even this phrase which puts it out there—is so difficult to get moving again, so one should try in advance to keep it alive while it's still in the process of coming to be, in oneself. It must keep on *originating*, that's what matters. One should never, never let it become something finished.
But how can anyone do this? (167)

This is precisely the question asked by women writers I mark as creating feminist, rather than feminine, discourse. How to unfix things? How to strip down or make moving the traditional or finished literary forms so that everything is always new? One way feminist discourse does this is through its confrontational stance. Feminist discourse is noted for its attack on the authority of language as well as the authority of experience as these are delimited for us by our culture. In feminist discourse, female experience is given centrality rather than accorded the usual marginality, as is the continuum of female experience (and also male experience with women). Similarly, each feminist text should question the authority and order of language, its capabilities for self-expression and its uses, the power of language to name, fix, or erase. Each text is, then, not only social representation but also ideological criticism since each reveals what is rarely seen in hegemonic discourse—woman as self-informing subject. Until recently, women writers have addressed these issues by appropriating conventional or traditional forms, such as local color fiction or the novel of manners, in order to pull out of line the boundaries of such discourse, in order to question traditional ways and means of representation, interpretation, being. Some women writers defer to or lose themselves in hegemonic discourse; others maintain difference by continuous confrontation. Even confrontation can be effected in different ways. We can easily see the variance between female discourse, as Elizabeth Cady Stanton called it (Huf 19), and feminist discourse when we contrast works such as Fanny Fern's *Ruth Hall* and Louisa May Alcott's *Work*. The titles alone indicate divergence of concerns. Both texts ask, "What's a *poor* girl to do?" Fern's text is closer to sentimental fiction, idealizing the struggle of one particular working girl who, because she is good in every possible way, is rewarded. She finds her place in the world and is enriched in the process. Alcott's text, on the other hand, is social fiction which exposes a continuum of complex and highly problematic social relations, offering in the end the possibility of a radically altered community, one based not on a romantic vision of reincorporation but on the making of a new dialectic. There is, of course, a thin line in feminist discourse between art and propaganda, between the aesthetic representation of possibility rather than the call for the utter necessity of making everything new in particular ways, but then, feminist discourse is moral art, methexis rather than mimesis.

Kate Chopin and Edith Wharton are not, to be precise, feminist writers. Neither woman aligned herself with the feminist movements of her day, nor did either label herself a feminist. Each did, however, produce what one might call, for want of a better term, female moral art in works that focus relentlessly on the dialectics of social relations and the position of woman therein. Their work stands as a clear link between nineteenth- and twentieth-century literary and cultural sensibilities as well as a critique of social theories and practices. As Jerome Klinkowitz writes, critics should be aware that "there is a very attractive pattern in Kate Chopin's development as a writer that reflects in microcosm the larger movement in American literature from romanticism and local color to realism and naturalism" (39); similarly, as Amy Kaplan argues, there is a need to "reassess Wharton's place in American literary history not as an antimodernist or a woman writer alone, but as a professional author who wrote at the intersection of the mass market of popular fiction, the tradition of women's literature, and a realistic movement which developed in an uneasy dialogue with twentieth-century modernism" (65–66). Chopin and Wharton were two of the first major American women writers to react against both the established dicta of "feminine" or sentimental fiction as well as the strictures of genteel and regionalist fiction. They reappropriated and transformed old forms in order to conceptualize the new content of their socially and morally responsive and responsible concerns. This is seen in their general themes: the individual's revolt against the inequalities manifest in genteel or bourgeois society; the decay of such a society and its replacement with the new money class and ethics of twentieth-century industrial entrepreneurs; the role of social determinism in class and personal crises; and the conflict between individual aspirations and social duty. It is also seen in their subversive renderings of traditional social and literary conventions and characterizations of social securities, limitations, and types, a discursive practice that Trinh T. Minh-ha describes as "the modernist project at its *nascent* stage: the radical calling into question, in every undertaking, of everything that one tends to take for granted" (40). In particular, they effected a new perspective on their societies' cult of true womanhood, a cultural signifier central to early twentieth-century American literature and an ideological formulation still of major concern today.

It is a given that literature in itself can offer only a somewhat obscure critique of bourgeois ethics—that is, if it is to maintain its literary nature and not descend into mere polemic; one might look to the work of Raymond Williams, Fredric Jameson, and John Goode for such discussion of text as social criticism. Both Chopin and Wharton were concerned in the main with producing art as they defined it. At the same time, in their social fiction, they implicitly stated their social critique in similar and stealthy fashion: both authors construct their major works around the modern alienated individual—either a specific woman or a specific man who perceives specific women as ideological types—on the verge of class rejection or ejection, offering alternatives, albeit tentative ones, to self-abnegation and social compromise. In their literature of protest, Chopin and Wharton spoke of and to the woman question through these characters, writing both realistic and critical portrayals of American women and the men who would love women in search of selfhood. Their work is thus part of the first modern female literary discourse in America, one in which women's experience is given cen-trality and expression.

An issue of immediate concern in the study of women writers is the reexamination of their works within the proper historical and cultural contexts. This can be effected by careful research in areas usually considered supplementary to literary criticism: ideology, economics, science, and so on. It is, of course, only a first step to place the work in its temporal reality; we obviously read the work from our time and in its textual non-time, but we should also attempt to do justice to the writer's intent and critical expectations. One must "enter" the text, as recent critics would have it, but one need not force such entry. It is, then, crucial to clarify how one enters and for what purpose.

One such entry point into the works of Chopin and Wharton is to focus on their representations of subjectivity and difference. To do so, one must seek elaboration and analysis of not only cultural constructs and imperatives—received ideas such as the ideology of true womanhood—but also the specificity of woman's experience and art. Even though Virginia Woolf's questions "Ah, but what is 'herself'? I mean what is a woman?" have yet the same answer, "I assure you, I do not know" (60), the critic can begin, as Mary Jacobus points out, the process of analyzing "the extent to which representation oppresses women to the ways in which it may be challenged from within and transformed by women themselves" (7). In other words, while elaboration of difference continues, the literary critic can study the causality of difference: the material reality of difference and the processes by which difference is expressed and given power by women artists.

In his *The Archaeology of Knowledge*, Michel Foucault writes of the problems facing critics who seek reinterpretation of history and culture:

> we must reconstitute another discourse, rediscover the silent murmuring, the inexhaustible speech that animates from within the voice that one hears, re-establish the tiny, invisible text that runs between and sometimes collides with them. The analysis of thought is always allegorical in relation to the discourse that it employs. Its question is unfailingly: what was being said in what was said? (27–28)

Jacobus, in her "Difference of View," places equal emphasis on seeing and speaking what is said; though she admits writing to be marginal and diffusive, she is also certain that there is a "quietly subversive power of writing, its power to destabilise the ground on which we stand" (18–19). Jacobus and critics who share this perspective seek the true history and discourse of women, those that decenter in crucial ways the hegemonic world view. They cannot as yet delimit woman's specificity, but they can analyze the process of woman's convergence with and recoil from masculinist (and feminine) discourse and worlds. Difference for them is no longer a term of dichotomy but of power, a term marking a continuum to which feminist criticism responds and in which it exists:

> *Difference* is redefined, not as male *versus* female—not as biologically constituted—but as a multiplicity, joyousness and heterogeneity which is that of textuality itself. Writing, the production of meaning, becomes the site both of challenge and Otherness; rather than (as in more traditional approaches) simply yielding the themes and representation of female oppression. *Difference*, in fact, becomes a traversal of the boundaries inscribed in Virginia Woolf's terms, but a traversal that exposes these very boundaries for what they are—the product of phallocentric discourse and of women's relation to patriarchal culture. Though necessarily working within "male" discourse, women's writing (in this scheme) would work ceaselessly to deconstruct it: to write what cannot be written. (12–13)

Further, as Foucault writes, "the problem is no longer one of tradition, of tracing a line, but one of division, of limits: it is no

longer one of lasting foundations, but one of transformations
that serve as new foundations, the rebuilding of foundations"
(5).

The following study will analyze the female discourse of Kate
Chopin and Edith Wharton and will look at that work as challenge and as difference. Both authors wrote primarily within set
boundaries—for example, local color fiction, the novel of manners—yet also inscribed therein a response to hegemonic language and ideology. Unlike comparable writers of their time,
their focus was not on individual, romanticized aesthetics or
portrayal of individual vices and virtues; both writers offer untenable representations of a particular, individual case in order
to criticize the social structures within which that individual experiences reality. Neither do they resemble the political ideo-
logues of their day; the deep structural and ideological
contradictions within their discourse are left purposely unresolved. Theirs is a nonpolemical but political art in which the
disruption of the rules of masculine/feminine discourse and of
the hegemonic world view is deeply but obviously embedded
within character, plot, and theme. The social fiction which they
produce thus denies ahistorical, totalized representations of
"truth"; instead, they write critical realism. They do so by relentlessly focusing their discourse on the traversals and boundaries as well as on the abyss of alienation into which their
characters might wander or fall.

The following chapters will discuss Chopin's and Wharton's
disintegrative visions, what Cynthia Griffin Wolff has called "the
fiction of limits" ("Kate Chopin" 133), what is essentially a fiction
of defeat. Specifically, as a means of speaking about relationships
of alienation and negation, analysis will begin with a brief examination of true womanhood ideology, a set of received ideas
about women that permeates Chopin's and Wharton's fiction and
world views. The remainder of this work will offer ideological
readings of their social fiction in which their characters, predominantly female, search for states of liminality in which they
might achieve, however momentarily, autonomy. Repeatedly,
these states of liminality are literally encoded into images of
characters positioned on the edge of an abyss. The abyss then
becomes a repository of multiple meanings, simultaneously rep-

resenting that outside the self, society's sink of immorality, and that within the self to which one surrenders in a final act of self-effacement or self-desire. This recurrent image of the everpresent abyss calls attention to life experienced on the boundaries, those between public and private spheres, between class rejection and ejection, between social incorporation or self-compromise, and self-alienation or self-expression. The liminal position of their characters seen in these works presages that of the modernists' deratiocinated individuals wandering the wasteland in a permanent state of alienation. It also bespeaks with intense drama the particular precariousness of becoming a woman, in Simone de Beauvoir's term (301), the costs involved in such ideological self-construction. Unlike recent feminist criticism which celebrates the position of marginality, their works elaborate the traumatic experience of those who suffer Wharton's *"vertige de l'abîme"* or who drown in Chopin's "abysses of solitude" so that the psychomachia be concluded (*Collected Short Stories* II, 122; *Complete Works* 893).

Chopin's and Wharton's female discourse, then, will be presented as radical art in that it "dares and defies" that which is both alienating and destructive (Chopin, *Complete Works* 946). As will be argued, theirs is a fiction of limits in which, as Jacobus writes, "the transgression of literary boundaries—moments when structures are shaken, when language refuses to lie down meekly, or the marginal is brought into sudden focus, or intelligibility itself refused—reveal not only the conditions of possibility within which women's writing exists, but what it would be like to revolutionise them" (16).

2

The Ideology of True Womanhood

The ideology of true womanhood, the cult of domesticity, and the separation of private and public spheres were not original nineteenth-century formulations and practices. The hegemonic status of this socio-sexual ideology had its foundations in long-standing philosophical and scientific beliefs in the natural inferiority of women coupled with, in America at least, the development of modern capitalist theories and practices. It is indeed romantic to imagine that colonial or preindustrial American women suffered no subordination of self and will. To the contrary, early democratic statemakers such as Thomas Jefferson, for example, made clear that three classes would always be excluded from power: children, slaves, and women. In addition, careful historical analysis of patriarchal cultures reveals the well-promoted conceptualization, objectification, and institutionalization of woman as lesser beings, as "other," as secondary adjunct to man. One need only skim through a work such as Rosemary Agonito's *History of Ideas on Woman* to discover the pervasiveness of such sexual and social theories in western culture, and one might look to Luce Irigaray's texts for a more modern account. What is notable about nineteenth-century American true womanhood theories is the complex and explicit codification of such socio-sexual ideology. This formalization clearly served distinct functions in a time of cataclysmic change, which saw the rise of industrial capitalism, the emergence of a strict and, for the mid-

dle class, necessary class system, the separation of economy from
the home and the consequent breakdown of traditional family
structures. Stephanie Coontz argues that such changes called for
a concerted "attempt to limit the transformation of personal
relations into commodity relations, to reserve one arena of life
free from the competition, conflicts, and insecurities of an ex-
panding capitalist democracy" (210). The very real possibility of
familial and cultural degeneration, the theoretical and actual
bifurcation of social life into two spheres—home and marketplace, the antediluvian construct of woman as inferior being
grafted on to the more modern one of woman as commodity/
object, all these affected the highly prescriptive and sometimes
oppressive true womanhood abstraction and actuality, the effects
of which postmodern culture still suffers.

Social historians as varied as Nancy Cott, Carroll Smith-
Rosenberg, Carl Degler, and Stephanie Coontz agree on the
central importance of true womanhood ideology to nineteenth-
century American social and economic transformation if not on
its value or cost to individuals—particularly women, of course—
and to the social collective. The majority would agree, however,
that the ideology of true womanhood was simultaneously an
attempt at social acculturation of men and women into a class
system and an increasingly suspect set of idealizations that called
into question all American progressive social theory. The tension
between abstract ideology or social expectations and actual social
practices becomes explosive by Chopin's and Wharton's time,
and this tension is at the heart of their social fiction.

The prescriptive component of true womanhood ideology can
be summarized in a few words. As are most ideological formulations, the doctrine of true womanhood was boldly simplistic in
its commandments. Woman, in essence, was to be preserver of
culture, the sympathetic and supportive bridge between the private realm of the home and the almost exclusively male world
of the public marketplace, herself the finest product of capitalism. She was to embody and to maintain social stability in a
volatile time of class struggle and economic amorality/immorality
through the nurturance of her womanhood self, her family, and
her sense of virtue. She was also to provide a haven of beauty,
grace, and refuge for the makers of this new world: her men.

Ralph Waldo Emerson in his lecture entitled "Woman
in support of woman's right to the vote, defines the
between the sexes as follows:

> Man is the will, and Woman the sentiment. In this ship of humanity,
> Will is the rudder, and Sentiment the sail: when Woman affects to steer,
> the rudder is only a masked sail. When women engage in any art or
> trade, it is usually as a resource, not as a primary object. The life of the
> affections is primary to them, so that there is usually no employment
> or career which they will not with their own applause and that of society
> quit for a suitable marriage. And they give entirely to their affections,
> set their whole fortune on the die, lose themselves eagerly in the glory
> of their husbands and children. (407)

The basic tenet, then, was the old one: " 'Man is a doer, an actor.
Woman reacts, she reflects rather than creates, is the moon to
his sun' " (Welter 77). That basic formulation was made new,
however, by its added fillip of accountability; as Stephanie
Coontz points out, "in its very insistence on the separation of
work and home, the cult of domesticity brought barter into the
realm of private life. Woman had to convince man that her love
was sufficient reward for her keep" (217–218).

The complementary behavioral code was equally straightforward. Barbara Welter in her seminal essay entitled "The Cult of
True Womanhood: 1820–1860" delineates it succinctly as a system of principles affording prizes or punishments:

> The attributes of True Womanhood, by which a woman judged herself
> and was judged by her husband, her neighbors and society, could be
> divided into four cardinal virtues—piety, purity, submissiveness and
> domesticity. Put them all together and they spelled mother, daughter,
> sister, wife—woman. Without them, no matter whether there was fame,
> achievement or wealth, all was ashes. With them she was promised
> happiness and power. (21)

Furthermore, a true woman "was destined to bring comfort and
beauty into man's life and to combat his more sensual nature
and the materialism of business" (57). Both Louise Michele Newman's collection *Men's Ideas/Women's Realities:* Popular Science,
1870–1915 and Stephanie Coontz's *The Origins of Private Life*

argue persuasively on how well-promoted and maintained such a view of woman was as well as how it permeated all classes until well after the turn of the century. Only then, at what Coontz calls "the apex of the doctrine of separate spheres" (252) would Coventry Patmore name the true woman and Virginia Woolf contest against her as the Angel in the House.

These precepts were supported by religious beliefs concerning woman's greater susceptibility to grace, and thus moral superiority, because of her emotive, supra-rational nature as well as scientific theories that "proved" woman's physical and mental inferiority to men. In brief, as Sheila M. Rothman writes in *Woman's Proper Place*, "the ideology rendered them at once incompetent and competent, broken and whole, to be pitied and to be emulated. But whatever the contradictions in this perspective, they disappeared in one grand edict: Women had better stay very much in their own sphere. They did not belong in the world of men" (26). Women might be angels upon whom the continuation of the race depended, but men would always be their gods.

One immediate and serious limitation of true womanhood ideology was that it "provided no way for people to resist or challenge the reorganization of work, the spread of the market, or the constriction of economic and social obligations. The domestic family may have attempted to shield its members from the corruptions and insecurities of capitalist *exchange*, but it never expressed any opposition to the dynamics of capitalist *production*" (Coontz 212). Further, it was an expression of white middle-class interests. Even though it played upon the desires for security, ones which appealed to all classes in its focus on the "family as a stable haven" (Coontz 262), it did not reflect the immediate or potential reality of lower class or immigrant women or, indeed, of some middle-class women themselves. It purposely did not acknowledge the growing work force of women, did not sanction professionalism and careerism for women, did not accept any notion of reality as superior to its own theoretical formulations, even though class aspirations and sharply delineated classes were at the core of the ideological model. True womanhood ideology is extremely conservative, then, in that it both "obscured the growing class distinctions among American families" (Coontz

216) and erased all specificity of difference between women in its reinscription of essential difference, its argument resting upon "some essence of womanhood that applies equally to all women" (Newman xxvi). At the same time, it both necessitated and justified the emergent class structuring. Further, it itself called for a microcosmic enactment of capitalist principles just as it applauded hierarchicalization, even though it simultaneously romanticized to the point of denial the inherent contradictions between capitalism in practice and democracy in theory within both the private and public spheres. Lawrence J. Friedman writes in his *Inventors of the Promised Land* that while the true womanhood doctrine was meant "to reconcile the irreconcilable" on both the individual and collective level, it failed utterly to do so (109). The true woman's home was, as Stephanie Coontz remarks, far from being "a refuge from the work world"; instead, "it was the shallow pool in which mothers first taught their children to swim in the waters of capitalist production—warning them to beware of sharks but still encouraging them to get their feet wet" (267). More pointedly, as Harriet Martineau noted after her American travels in 1837, "The Americans have, in the treatment of women fallen below, not only their own democratic principles, but the practice of some parts of the Old World" (2: 226).

Further, though the doctrine was intended to reconcile the irreconcilable, it could not even disguise its own schizophrenic prescriptions. For example, democratic principles as well as social aspiration were implicitly upheld by the theory. To be a true woman required financial stability; wealth was simultaneously the support and prize of the lady and, later, the woman of leisure. Because woman could respectfully gain money and "leisure" only through marriage, her first "work" was to construct or to create a true woman self in accordance with ideological paradigms. Ideally, every woman had equal opportunity to advance to the true calling of wife and lady; she need only incorporate ideological dicta into her presentation of self, fit herself to the desired and desirable pattern. The theories of true womanhood were thus propounded as egalitarian and democratic. In reality, relationships between the sexes reflected basic capitalist principles of supply and demand in the marriage marketplace, self-ag-

ient, unequal opportunity, and the preservation of
nctions and inequalities, a reality vigorously critiqued
)cial critics as Thorstein Veblen. The received romantic
idea of marriage, as Barbara Welter writes, was also patently
false:

Marriage was a demonstrable step up in the hierarchy of society, one
of the few ways in which a woman could make such a move. Marriage
could provide for a woman the improved economic and social benefits
which men received through education, speculation, the professions,
business, and marriage. Most American girls believed that this new state
automatically brought happiness, because they believed that to marry
for anything but the purest love was unworthy of their sex and nature.
This freedom of choice was more apparent than real; most American
girls married within their own class, religion, and geographic background (8).

Furthermore, women by the very prescriptions of the behavioral
code could not actively engage in the competitiveness of the
marriage marketplace; to do so would be to prove unwomanly.
Rather, woman must remain passive concerning her one opportunity for the American Dream. As Welter also points out,
"the major events of a girl's life were to be products of arrangement and fate, not of intellect and will, and she was expected to
passively await them, as she awaited the arrival of her love" (17).
The would-be true woman was thus denied even her first and
only work: the effecting of a socially valuable self, however alienating that transformation of self be. Nor should she pursue
work of any other kind. Charlotte Perkins Gilman, among others,
analyzed this double bind in her many works, arguing that as
long as the separate spheres were maintained by denying woman
access to the world of business and by devaluing the domestic
work she provided gratis, woman would also remain at best a
dependent, at worst a slave, an object of property rather than a
human being.

What then was the positive value or appeal of true womanhood
ideology to women if they appeared to be at the mercy of fate,
always already subject(ed) to man's desire? Stephanie Coontz
draws attention to the fact that "theories of woman's separate
nature were not simply imposed on women but developed as a

dialectic between men and women seeking to explain and come to terms with their new positions in society." She goes on to argue that "the assignment of all women to a special place by virtue of their sex held out the promise of privilege to women who had had no opportunities to be exceptional as individuals" (219). The ideology did codify a system of moral values and did prescribe a code of behavior that was advantageous in some ways to some women. For example, Carl Degler as well as other social historians theorizes that the ideological tenets put into practice allowed women more control in their sexual relationships and, therefore, in childbearing and rearing. However, the ideology of womanhood did not, as Coontz also notes, in this way pose a "serious challenge to male privilege and in certain areas even gave it a new lease on life" (220). Indeed, because "the cult of domesticity validated the economic and political processes that removed law from the private sphere and morality from the public sphere, supposedly giving men 'rights' and women 'virtue,'" the new ethics inadvertently justified a natural double standard (213). Further, since "the conception of virtue took on private, feminine qualities—qualities that served less as the basis of public behavior than as the antithesis of it," woman could not exact from men reform of their behavior (231). Submissiveness, after all, was also a given "privilege." As has already been argued, the ideology merely promised a potential accrual of social and economic securities; it did not, however, challenge the necessary inequalities within class or social relations. Thus the "promise" inherent in the ideology would prove of little value to those women not already in possession of secure class and financial status by virtue of their being born with these and with which they could effect the commodification and marketing of the self.

A second ostensible appeal of this socio-sexual ideology was that it seemed to give some degree of social control to woman, making her powerful within her own sphere of the home. Within the circumscribed limits of her domestic realm, the true woman was able indirectly to influence and to maintain culture and society through the sacrifice of her self for the education of future generations and the spiritual upliftment of men. Domesticity did indeed become woman's art and work; Catharine Beecher's treatises, for example, show the extreme seriousness with which women took up their roles as educators and moral guardians. However, the contradictions within the ideology were, again, eventually revealed as in conflict with these purported social ends. If women were to educate, they must themselves leave their sphere, go into the world and be educated; if women were to maintain a moral society, they must have direct influence on social theories and practices. Further, if women were truly spiritually superior, they could not in good conscience remain within their sphere passively contented. The ideological formulation thus both called for and denied power to women, but however elusive women's power might be, it could be wielded to great advantage at particular moments. One may look to Harriet Beecher Stowe's *Uncle Tom's Cabin* for such an instance, discovering there what influence a true woman could have on socioeconomic policy. One must also note that her work was influential precisely because Stowe did not forward socio-economic arguments but focused instead on the moral issues the practice of slavery denied. In other words, the basic tenets of the code allowed momentary enactments of power but also required strict limitations of the ways in which power might be engaged and the ends to which such power might be addressed.

Finally, the ideology of true womanhood advocated specific social roles for women—that is, possible self-fulfillment as mother, wife, and lady free from the toil and exploitation of the marketplace. The romanticism of this premise has already been discussed, but the consequent alienation of private self from public self needs further elaboration. As has been made clear by numerous critics, here Barbara J. Harris, "the woman who approached the ideal obliterated her sense of self and virtually existed only in relation to others" (34). The ideological demands, in other words, necessitated that woman exploit a male ideal of Womanhood and thus erase her own individual specificity and self-will. For example, as Caroline Hazard, president of Wellesley College in 1900, sermonized, a woman's first lesson was to learn social obedience and to practice self-effacement: "Obedience implies absolute unselfishness. One gives up one's own will, one gives up one's own desire of expression, one puts all one's powers at the command of another" (13). The life, then, of a true woman was to be one of submissive sacrifice, self-martrydom, profound effacement of self for the promotion of an amoral, depersonalized world. The dreams and aspirations that she was to cultivate and sustain, the roles she was to fulfill, the influence she was to wield, all were barren, predicated on denial of self, denial of women as individuals, denial of the American Dream of men and women together creating the new Promised Land. Female reality was clearly, then, one of severe limits and inevitable compromise.

However, ideology, no matter how powerfully argued, is not synonymous with absolute reality. Mary Kelley writes in *Woman's Being, Woman's Place*:

Woman neither totally fulfilled the stereotype nor remained completely immune from its dictates. Instead, the relationship between prescription and behavior was an extraordinarily complex one which varied with individual and historical circumstances. Equally important, . . . women were not only affected by the process of socialization, but they affected that process as well. In short, women were active participants as well as passive recipients in the elaboration of culture. (89)

One result of the ideology of true womanhood was that an increasing number of women did begin to perceive themselves as a specific group, a first step in a new social consciousness. Women also became aware of new types of social responsibility, this realization stemming in part from ideological concepts of female moral superiority. Indeed, since the true womanhood prescriptions were so innately contradictory, both feminists and anti-feminists alike could support its tenets and use these for their own purposes. Anti-feminists had only to follow the code to the letter; feminists read between the letters, subverting further irreconcilable contradictions, slowly moving into the public sphere and beginning pragmatic social reforms under the guise of spiritual and ethical guardianship. One tenet, however, that neither group could easily negotiate was the double standard and the subordination of women to male interests and desires, women's self-objectification as sexual property.

Despite the extreme distances thus inscribed between men and women, for the majority, the myths of male supremacy and feminine inferiority were accepted as universal "truths," so

deeply inculcated as to approach nonconsciousness. Sandra and
Daryl Bem in their "Case Study of a Nonconscious Ideology:
Training the Woman to Know Her Place" speculate that beliefs
and attitudes about women held both by men and by women
make up the most pervasive and tenacious nonconscious ideology in America. The Bems argue that the reason for this nonconsciousness is an inability to conceptualize alternate social
realities or world views (89–99). The social historian might note,
for instance, the transmutation of the cult of true womanhood,
supposedly regnant only from 1820–1860, into more modern
forms used similarly to justify economic and social inequalities
between the sexes and classes. Betty Friedan, for example, theo-
rized that true womanhood was reborn after World War II as
"the feminine mystique." Again women were forced out of the
public sphere and back into the private. Even more recent, and
more dangerous, is the promotion of total womanhood ideology
by conservative and fundamentalist groups in the United States
and their attempts to reinstitute and institutionalize through law
the doctrine of separate spheres and sexual inequality. Yet, some
women did attain a deep consciousness of the costs necessitated
by ideological complicity, a profound awareness of the effects
of cataclysmic social change, the consequent reordering of values
and power. And, simultaneously, the hegemonic power-wielders
were quite aware of the subversive power of these women among
whom stand Chopin and Wharton.

Barbara Welter insists that "no matter what later authorities
claimed, the nineteenth century knew that girls *could* be ruined
by a book. . . . Books which attacked or seemed to attack woman's
accepted place in society were regarded as equally dangerous"
(34). Helen Papashvily in *All the Happy Endings* has argued that
domestic and sentimental fiction—for example, Fanny Fern's
Ruth Hall or Louisa May Alcott's *Work*—was a first literary reaction against and subversion of true womanhood ideology.
However, the majority of sentimental or domestic novelists, as
overviews such as that by Nina Baym suggest, offered romantic,
conservative responses to ideological self-constitution and social
expectations; they did so, in part, to remain marketable. It is not
until the late nineteenth and early twentieth century that readers
were confronted with the clearly dangerous works of the new

social realists and critics who defied social givens, received ideas, and reactionary belief in magically happy endings. In these works, as Virginia Woolf effected in her own case, women writers first killed the Angel in the House in themselves and then levelled a continual barrage of words against the ideological angels in their fiction (Woolf 57–63).

Just so do Chopin's and Wharton's books, for their major works center on women within their societies doing battle with both ideological theory and practice, women who envision, however vaguely, another way of being. Florence Nightingale, no feminist but no angel either, wrote in her "Cassandra":

Women dream till they have no longer the strength to dream; those dreams against which they so struggle, so honestly, vigorously, and conscientiously, and so in vain, yet which are their life, without which they could not have lived; those dreams go at last. All their plans and visions seem vanished, and they know not where, gone and they cannot recall them. They do not even remember them. And they are left without the food either of reality or of hope. (49)

By representing in detail the dreams, ideological disbeliefs, and social realities of both women and men, Chopin and Wharton offer readers both criticism of what was and implicit visions of what could be, alternative worlds imagined if only through self-annihilation.

3

Kate Chopin's Life and Art

Kate Chopin was born in 1850 of Irish and French parents in the slave city of St. Louis, spent her married years in the deep South, and lived to see the emancipation, the industrial transformation of feudal plantation life, and the arrival of seemingly "every facet of the world's achievement, in industry, science, literature and the arts" to her world before her death on 22 August 1904 (Seyersted 185). Her extended family on her mother's side was an established Creole clan; her immigrant father was a successful merchant and railroad founder. After his accidental death in 1855, she was brought up by a French matriarchy of three generations of related Creole women, all widows. Her family supported the Confederacy during the Civil War, and Kate's activities earned her the nickname of "St. Louis' Littlest Rebel." She was schooled outside the home and received the necessary education of a lady, coming out as a debutante in 1868.

In 1870, she married Oscar Chopin, a Creole who was distantly related to her, moving first to New Orleans and then, after the failure of his business, to the Chopin family plantations in northwest Louisiana, where she led a genteel and somewhat independent life as his châtelaine. Before the age of thirty, she had had five sons and one daughter. At thirty-two, she was widowed, and after overseeing the plantations for a year, she returned to St. Louis and life within the matriarchy. As Helen Taylor points out, "the influence of the women of the family is rightly seen by her biographers as positive and liberating. However, in many ways the strong Catholic piety and religious fervor of her female relatives must have stifled Chopin, especially as she grew older and also became a strong independent widow with apparently no intention of remarrying" (141). After her mother's death in 1885, and at the urging of a family friend, she turned to serious and salable writing. Between 1888 and 1904, she produced three novels, some one hundred stories, various sketches, poems, a one-act play, and several critical essays, many of these written in her living rooms while she was surrounded by her children. She was considered a successful and fashionable writer before *The Awakening*, written after her grandmother's death in 1897; after 1899, she produced little work, and much of it remains unpublished.

Her writing career and deep interest in literature began, of course, long before her widowhood. Contrary to contemporary reports, she was not a spontaneous and aesthetically naive writer, one of the legion of "scribbling ladies." Her mental preparation and study of technique were in fact quite extensive; Per Seyersted and Emily Toth, notably, offer detailed, verifiable, and conjectural background on her artistic development and influences (see Seyersted's biography, Toth's dissertation, and their *A Kate Chopin Miscellany*).

Chopin, unlike many women of her time, read and read widely. She seems not to have suffered the restrictions of censorship Wharton would. In addition to knowledge of written texts, Chopin was steeped in oral story-telling by her great-grandmother who favored historical and fanciful tales of those who defied social expectations. Chopin also kept various diaries and commonplace books, and from these one can reconstruct in part her self-education as a writer.

By the age of twenty, Chopin had studied and at times critiqued "such authors as Dante, Cervantes, Corneille, Racine, Molière, Mme. de Staël, Chateaubriand, Goethe, Coleridge, Jane Austen, Charlotte Brontë, and Longfellow" (Seyersted 25). She was also drawn to literature of rebellion, particularly that focusing on the woman question; her private notes contain numerous quotations on the subject, some with marked copy but none with her own commentary. One sees the influence of her radical tastes in reading translated into writing in her earliest extant piece, "Emancipation. A Life Fable" written in late 1869 or early 1870 and left unpublished in her lifetime. It is not surprising, moreover, that she then gave up writing for nearly twenty years; the content of this fable and the progress of her self-education show her consciousness of the marked difference between liberal ideology or rhetoric and the possibility of radical practice. For half of her own life, she was a dutiful and seemingly contented daughter, wife, and mother; she spent the final half writing at her best about women who could neither make the leap she had toward personal liberation nor content themselves with the traditional and, to them, restrictive roles for women advocated by society.

Five years after her husband's death, Chopin began her career as writer with a public. By then she had read widely in science, philosophy, and literature, works which influenced not only her private philosophy but also the public expression of the same through her fiction. Her earliest stories show a marked concern with psychological realism, especially psychological portraiture of women at odds with the world, and distanced or amoral narration. This also holds true for her first novel, *At Fault* (1890), which she published and promoted at her own expense. Parts of the novel are preferable to the whole, but it is notable in that the highly volatile subject of divorce is treated in a radically nonmoralistic fashion. This novel was ignored by critics who, perhaps, preferred Chopin as short story artist though she herself denied a specialization in and preference for one literary form over the other.

Nevertheless, after the rejection of a second novel, Chopin did seem to return to the short story form. Between 1891-1894, she wrote some forty stories and sketches. She published these first in both mainstream and less traditional magazines, later collecting twenty-three pieces in *Bayou Folk* (1894). By then she was firmly established with the public and critical press as a local colorist. This reputation was maintained with the reception of *A Night in Acadie* (1897), which collected pre–1896 stories, even though few of the stories were obviously local color pieces but many were, instead, small *Awakening*s. So too were most of her

stories written in 1897. It is evident that Chopin intended her
third novel to be her most polished and deliberate work, and
that many of her earlier pieces, though significant in their own
way, were partial, rough sketches for this final masterpiece.

Equally important at this point in her career was the publication of a series of short critical essays. Chopin was extremely
reticent about disclosing her specific techniques and thematic
focus or of offering herself as artistic model. She also was loath
to suggest any interpretation or view of her work which might
be taken as definitive; for Chopin, "truth rests upon a shifting
basis and is apt to be kaleidoscopic" (697). One can conjecture,
however, that her intent in these essays was to show her literary
influences and sensibility, if obliquely, and to position herself
within specific literary movements, if, again, only by implication.

What is immediately evident is that Chopin did not consider
herself one with the regionalists or local color artists. In her
"The Western Association of Writers," she makes clear that the
limited scope of those writers denied the true subject of art:
"human existence in its subtle, complex, true meaning, stripped
of the veil with which ethical and conventional standards have
draped it" (691). Furthermore, in her review entitled " 'Crum-
bling Idols' by Hamlin Garland," she evinced little sympathy for
the propagandistic aspect of social problem fiction; neither did
she show any favor toward didactic or sentimental fiction.
Rather, she seems closer to what Adrienne Rich noted recently
as the design and intent of feminist writers: "to render those
parts of the truth that we are best able to embody, knowing that
others are at work on other parts of the project" (192). Chopin
similarly saw art as a form of individual expression of individually determined truths, some individual truths being shared by
many. For her and for her favored authors, art was a form of
self-expression that was seemingly amoralistic in its choice of
subjects but also extremely radical in that she felt there were no
subjects true to the life of the writer that could or should not be
presented. Her appreciation of Maupassant, Whitman, Jewett,
and Mary E. Wilkins, in particular, reveal her affinity for and
with practitioners of intensely controlled technique—particularly in terms of characterization, plot development, and point

of view—and with makers of a new, modern fiction of passion, psychological insight, and critical realism.

Chopin would publicly maintain that her writing was "the spontaneous expression of impressions gathered goodness knows where" and that she was "completely at the mercy of unconscious selection" (722). These accounts may have been a reaction against critics and their invasion of her privacy; or, as Chopin also writes, "the victim cannot take herself too seriously" (723). However, her private diaries and some few comments in her essays point to the contrary: that she was highly aware of her own style and limitations, that she avidly studied and imitated the technique of Maupassant and Jewett. In fact, she identified so strongly with Maupassant that she translated several of his stories, available in Thomas Bonner, Jr.'s *The Kate Chopin Companion,* and disguised herself "as a gentleman" in her "Confidences" written in praise of Maupassant's tales. One discovers in this essay the source of her desire for such self-identification in her summation of Maupassant's achievement:

Here was life, not fiction; for where were the plots, the old fashioned mechanism and stage trapping that in a vague, unthinking way I had fancied were essential to the art of story making. Here was a man who had escaped from tradition and authority, who had entered into himself and looked out upon life through his own being and with his own eyes; and who, in a direct and simple way, told us what he saw. When a man does this, he gives us the best that he can; something valuable for it is genuine and spontaneous. (700–701)

She further imagines him saying to her, " 'if ever you are moved to write stories you can do no better than to imitate' " (701). Her "Impressions" of 1894 also indicates her aesthetic taste; for her, Wilkins' "*Pembroke* is the most profound, the most powerful piece of fiction of its kind that has ever come from the American press" (*Kate Chopin Miscellany* 90). That grim novel of passionate, unconventional love was adjudged by major critics as a crude, salacious local color piece; just so would Chopin's *The Awakening* be received in 1899. Chopin, in brief, did make clear the company she kept. When critics finally heard her voice, they consigned her and some of that company to a literary limbo.

Kate Chopin is perhaps best known for the critical damnation exercised against her. It is literary legend that critical and popular response to *The Awakening* killed her. One can certainly speculate that the attack on her work hastened her death, but such conjecture has little to do with literary criticism. It is, however, a significant fact that the critical onslaught in 1899 killed her literary reputation and destroyed her marketability and, hence, her chance at gaining an audience. One can also postulate that her pre–1899 criticism abetted in her literary demise. The response to her before *The Awakening* did not shore up her reputation and defenses for the battle to come.

Chopin at first was simply seen as another local colorist in a long line of southern writers of whom the greats had already been designated, notably Joel Chandler Harris and George Washington Cable. Even recent critics of regionalist literature include her in lists of authors, noting as an aside that she actually did not and does not fit the conventions or concerns of that genre. According to critics in Chopin's day, sentimental and regionalist women writers of the 1800s, with a few very important exceptions, were read as advocating traditional social models; the authors' limited experience or consciousness determined their choice of popular literary modes—romance and melodrama—and stressed acceptance of social duty and preservation of the past. Much local color fiction was criticized as profoundly reactionary in that it was seen as a looking backward for a golden age that had never existed. It served to deny progress, social transformation. This account, of course, is that of some leading critics and not, it should be emphasized, that of many writers or their readers. In fact, it is clear from Chopin's earliest stories that looking backward was not her intent nor that regionalist fiction was for her a limitation, but critics would not applaud this until long after her death. Instead, her contemporary critics avoided detailed analysis of her work and were content with offering impressions, suggestions, gracious compliments and various sketches of the woman writer at work. This type of analysis was undoubtedly considered adequate both as criticism and reportage in its time, and examples are readily available to modern critics in *A Kate Chopin Miscellany* (see, for instance, Sue V. Moore's authorized sketch or William Schuyler's review/interview, 111–119). Such appreciations offer valuable information and some random insights, but they certainly do not constitute a critical discourse capable of positioning Chopin as a major writer within the canon.

Chopin was also categorized early on as a mistress of the short story form but not of the novel. The negative impact of such labelling in her case is curious. Most major writers of the time worked with the short story form, and many of their short stories were considered works of art. Those of Chopin, as well as those of Jewett, Wilkins, and other women regionalist writers, usually were not, although they were acknowledged as highly popular reading. Perhaps again it was simply a question of who should be allowed entry into the American canon, one known until recently for its own limitations; or, perhaps, the pejorative critique suggested in the label of "woman short story writer" refers to Chopin's minimal production as a novelist. She rushed her first novel into print at her own expense, and copies were, no doubt, hard to come by because of its limited run. Even so, no major criticism on that novel appeared until very recently, and that critical neglect is less easy to discount. Further, publishers summarily rejected her second novel ostensibly because of its content. One might suspect an attempt on the part of those publishers to disregard Chopin the unprofitable novelist for Chopin the profitable short story writer. In any case, it was not until she was fully established as a short story writer that her third novel was accorded very critical attention.

This critical attention, of course, can now been seen as the nailing down of the coffin lid, occasioning as it did a reevaluation of her entire career. Earlier correspondence between Chopin and her various editors reveals that she had been asked in several instances to rewrite stories considered too indelicate or immoral for her audience. Certain pieces were also refused; others were never even submitted; a second novel was destroyed after Chopin's fruitless attempts to find a publisher. Yet even this correspondence—and critical muttering—could not have prepared Chopin for the critical reaction to *The Awakening*, nor can modern readers readily comprehend what can be called the hatchet job done on Chopin the writer and woman. Margaret Culley's excellent critical edition of the novel makes available a collection of contemporary reviews which are astounding for their rabidity, morbidity, intolerance, and venomous sexism. Chopin's portrayal of the sexual and social awakening of a woman clearly insulted or frightened both her audience and the literary establishment; the challenge of the book, the transformation effected within, boded ill if translated into the world outside the text. Chopin was castigated for writing unhealthy sex fiction, flawless but immoral art, a study in morbidity better suited to psychological textbooks, pornographic animalism which debased human nature, proved vulgar, corrupted, smelled (141–159). Perhaps the most interesting critical statement is that of the Providence *Sunday Journal* critic: "We are fain to believe that Miss Chopin did not herself realize what she was doing when she wrote it" (149). By late 1899, then, Chopin in the eyes of one critic was no longer even a quaint regionalist or a feminine Maupassant; she was not even Kate Chopin, or, at least, the one recognizable as such. An extraordinary incident of critical and personal erasure, this, one which foreshadowed decades of critical neglect.

Between 1900 and 1930, attention was paid to some of Chopin's work but, again, only within studies on regionalists and short story writers. Daniel S. Rankin's *Kate Chopin and Her Creole Stories*, his dissertation published in 1932, offered new biographical material and a collection of her stories, but his analysis of her works and, notably, of *The Awakening* did not offer significantly radical rereadings. Little major work then appeared until Cyrille Arnavon's 1953 introduction to a French edition of *The Awakening*, retitled as *Edna*; this important piece, however, was virtually unavailable to critics until its translation and inclusion in *A Kate Chopin Miscellany* (168–188). Chopin remained until recently a shadow figure on the edge of the canon.

Contemporary Chopin critics can virtually recite a litany naming those scholars who beginning in the 1960s reawakened interest in Chopin. Again, Margaret Culley's critical edition of *The Awakening* is invaluable in its overview of major criticism on Chopin written in the 1960s and 1970s. Reviewing that body of critical thought, one finds essays of bewilderment concerning Chopin's silencing and neglect, those of, for example, Larzer Ziff, Edmund Wilson, and Stanley Kauffmann. One also sees serious analysis of Chopin's manipulation of form and content in the essays of Kenneth Eble, Robert Cantwell, Lewis Leary, and Donald Ringe. Most important for critics and readers alike, of course, is Per Seyersted's 1969 edition of *The Complete Works of Kate Chopin* and, a decade later, the publication of *A Kate Chopin Miscellany* edited by Seyersted and Emily Toth. The body of work is, at last, made available, and critical interest intensifies, especially after the 1969 publication of Seyersted's *Kate Chopin: A Critical Biography*. *The Kate Chopin Newsletter* appears in 1975 under the editorship of Emily Toth, herself one of the leading Chopin scholars and whose dissertation and numerous articles move Chopin studies radically forward. Robert Arner's work, particularly that presented as the *Louisiana Studies* Spring 1975 issue, similarly argues for Chopin's importance as writer and social critic.

In the decade of the 1980s has come a veritable outpouring of critical Chopin studies, and because of that attention, Chopin's work is now routinely included in anthologies, *The Awakening* become required reading in numerous university courses. Seyersted's analytical biography remains a starting point for scholars as do the later critical overviews written by Peggy Skaggs and Barbara Ewell. The most recent criticism, much of which shows a concurrent interest in feminist theory and practice, is highly valuable in that it recognizes both Chopin's literary and ideological concerns. One can sample such views in *Approaches to Teaching Chopin's* The Awakening, edited by Bernard Koloski, or in *New Essays on* The Awakening, edited by Wendy Martin. While it is no longer a matter of debate whether Chopin be considered a potentially major literary figure, there is still a need for further work before it can be determined precisely in what position Chopin's social fiction stands in relation to canonic and feminist discourse. Anne Goodwyn Jones' excellent chapter on Chopin in her *Tomorrow Is Another Day* is such a new direction in critical analysis as are studies by Anna Shannon Elfenbein and Helen Taylor, which focus on issues of race and gender in Chopin's work. No doubt the publication of what promises to be the definitive critical biography by Emily Toth will also radically transform the trajectory of Chopin studies.

One insurpassable obstacle in Chopin studies, however, is the

fact that Chopin does not, in her critical essays, ever overtly state
her central subject or theme. Most critics, nevertheless, readily
agree that her major theme is the defiance of woman against
social convention and hegemonic ideology. Emily Toth, in her
dissertation, links Chopin with the domestic and plantation traditions but, more importantly, delineates the all-pervasiveness
of the woman question in the social criticism and fiction of the
day. Further, since the ideology of true womanhood was central
in Chopin's life, it is not surprising that this might be the major
impression or truth she would express. What is astonishing is
that she had the temerity to do so, to present implicit critiques
of social conventions and ideology within her fiction. Her subversive artistry can best be understood as an extension of her
private philosophy and pessimistic world view. She did not believe in either ethical absolutes or the total absence of ethics.
Neither did she see her world as necessarily progressive or ret-
rogressive. For Chopin, each individual—particularly each
woman—possessed infinite potential for self-fulfillment and
expression but also, at the same time, the greater possibility for
self-compromise and self-destruction. And these two faces of the
same coin were not purely determined by nature but also of
nurture: "Human impulses do not change and can not so long
as men and women continue to stand in the relation to one
another which they have occupied since our knowledge of their
existence began" (693). Her finest fiction, like Edith Wharton's,
posits the possibility of changing those relations. She does so by
presenting to the reader women who defy those longstanding
socio-sexual relations even though because of that defiance they
fall at last into abysses of solitude and self-alienation.

4

Kate Chopin's Social Fiction

Kate Chopin's fictional world encompasses all of the nineteenth-century South and is one contemporaneous with her life. She is writing, then, within a period of enormous transmogrification: the pre-capitalist, patriarchal plantation economy built on slavery giving way to industrialization of the land and economic assimilation of the South into a post-Civil War "united" state built on a new class system and based, in part, on the retention of a large working class and the subordination of women of all classes. Concomitantly, she addresses myths of nostalgia and progress, examining the seductive stasis of the old order and the uncertain authority of the new, as evinced both in the private and public spheres. In addition, she depicts social stratification—for example, the social, economic, and sexual segregation of Creoles, Arcadians, poor whites, frontierspeople, new money southerners, and blacks—as both the cause and effect of individual and collective alienation.

Her South is not the romantic vision put forth by many of her contemporary regionalist writers; instead, the real metamorphoses occurring in her time stand as constant background and touchstone to her major subject: the emergent selves of women defying the social securities and strictures of the old South, judging and being judged by the ideological parameters of the true womanhood code. Chopin writes across class and color lines portraying virtually every southern "type," but she, like Whar-

ton, focuses in her major works on her own class and sex: Creole
or upper middle-class society and the position of women within
it. The ideology of true womanhood is as basic to her work as
women are central within society.

It is common knowledge that the cult of domesticity and true
womanhood outlined earlier was particularly exaggerated in the
antebellum South. As historian Anne Firor Scott points out,
"Women, like slaves, were an intrinsic part of the patriarchal
dream" (53). Plantation life in order to be profitable necessitated
strict hierarchic systemization of all social/sexual relationships—
master/mistress to slave, man to woman—as well as ideological
justification for ruling class practices. The ideal southern woman
was not just an imaginary distortion of male demands but a
realizable construct of immense value to the patriarchy. To cite
Scott again, "Motherhood, happy families, omnipotent men, satisfied slaves—all were essential parts of the image of the organic
patriarchy." She goes on to say that "in none of these areas did
the image accurately depict the whole reality" (63). One can
argue, however, that women's lived reality was extremely limited,
subject as it was in multiple ways to hegemonic rule. More crucial
in the experience of many white southern women was their apprehension of the irreconcilable contradictions between ideological theory and social practice. The moral double standard
inherent within true womanhood tenets made glaringly apparent
the disparities between ideological abstraction and lived experience; in particular, "miscegenation was the fatal flaw in the
patriarchal doctrine" (Scott 59). Male sexual practices refuted
the hegemonic hierarchy, breaking down the distinction between
woman and slave; both nonracist and racist women felt the threat
of that breach. Furthermore, if women were to fulfill their ideological function as moral guardians, they could perhaps support
slavery as a system of labor, since slavery then is seen as an issue
of economics within the male sphere, but could not do so if that
system were also one based on physical and spiritual oppression,
since the maintenance of slavery then raised issues falling within
woman's sphere. For example, as noted earlier, Harriet Beecher
Stowe's *Uncle Tom's Cabin, or Life Among the Lowly* stands as a
model for the true womanhood literary response to unchristian
acts but not to slavery as a productive if exploitative system of

labor. Chopin evoked the slavery issue and woman's response to it in several stories—notably Désirée's Baby" and "La Belle Zoraïde," but in general, such catastrophic socioeconomic problems serve as background in her fiction to larger philosophical issues made comprehensible by their individualization. Chopin saw that for women of any color life in the antebellum and postbellum South was potentially abysmal. The struggle against cultural imperatives is a fierce one, made even more notable in Chopin's representation of it through her focus on states of liminality.

Cynthia Griffin Wolff, in her "Kate Chopin and the Fiction of Limits," points this out in her overview:

A majority of Chopin's fictions are set in worlds where stability or permanence is a precarious state: change is always threatened—by the vagaries of impassive fate, by the assaults of potentially ungovernable individual passions, or merely by the inexorable passage of time. More generally, we might say that Chopin construes existence as necessarily uncertain. (125)

More specifically and reinterpreting Wolff, one can see that because Chopin chose to portray women schooled in piety, purity, and passivity, she could not have produced anything other than a fiction of limits and, in many cases, of defeat. Social and sexual ideology which had never fully acknowledged the self-will and personal aspiration of women could prove only more alienating to the individual confronting the shifting reality of the old patriarchal order giving way to a modern, amoral world that yet maintained contradictory prescriptions concerning women. Within this shifting reality, there is seemingly no place for the inscription of woman's desire; or, as Wolff writes of Chopin, "what she sees is the ominous and insistent presence of the margin: the inescapable fact that even our most vital moments must be experienced on the boundary—always threatening to slip away from us into something else, into some dark, undefined contingency" (126). Indeed, in Chopin's world view and fiction, the marginalization of women's lives and desires, the consequent alienation of these individuals within and from their social collectives, becomes the central issue, the boundaries suddenly brought into sharp, clear focus.

As most critics point out, Chopin's earliest stories effectively delimit a range of responses to womanhood ideology and offer characterizations of women that will inform her entire opus. There is, in other words, a direct link between her earliest complete story "Emancipation. A Life Fable" (ca. 1869–1870) and *The Awakening* (1899); Chopin begins and ends with works that dare and defy, simultaneously deconstructing romantic rebellion and elucidating the pragmatics and penalties of particular individual revolts against society. Stories written by early 1891 set out in microcosm the grander pattern of Chopin's later literary explorations and effectively introduce all the central concerns therein: the awakening of woman to her true self (or selves) and the abysses of solitude or alienation into which that self wanders in her quest for fulfillment.

Chopin's women are not as easily compartmentalized as Wharton's: not for her the straightforward portrayal of ideologically stereotypical women—martyr, mistress, masterpiece. However, Chopin does make up her own continuum of females responding to ideology: woman as "true woman," a seemingly helpless being who is defined only through relationships to and with men; woman as outsider, an artist of a new world view; woman as dual self, a female precariously balanced between submission and self-will.

Chopin first created a patently romantic response to entrapment, a rebellion that is neither willful revolt nor, indeed, female or human in body or soul. Nonetheless, and even though it can be read as naive wish-fulfillment, the animal and animalistic fable of "Emancipation" cannot be denied its importance to Chopin's development. This early work acts as contrast to and kernel for *The Awakening*; further, it offers the sentimentalist, romantic response to life that Chopin will reconstruct, analyze, and then destroy in her later fiction.

In "Emancipation. A Life Fable," an animal born and bred in a cage moves from satisfied, solipsistic existence to isolation in and partial consciousness of a larger world. The male animal while entrapped is nurtured by "an invisible protecting hand" (37) and believes himself to be the center of the universe: the hand that feeds him and the light that warms him exist, he believes, only for those purposes. By chance his cage door is left open. Since he is a "pet" animal and also a creature without knowledge or consciousness, he cannot either close the door or ignore the intrusive effect on his world; more and more "Light" (37) shines in on him until he leaps out into it. Still without consciousness of his true self, "heedless that he is wounding and tearing his sleek sides" (37), he rushes into the world and experiences a sudden and dangerous sensuous awakening. He is no longer kept and cossetted but must now seek his own sustenance and discover his own substance. Despite his isolation and suffering, the animal remains in the world: "the cage remains forever empty!" (38)

Chopin's moral is clear: one must live in the world and be of it; one must discover a self in body (the senses) and in mind (Light) even though that quest be painful and, at first, disillusioning. However, Chopin's romantic means toward this radically open-ended statement are clearly unsophisticated choices. The first false note that points to her lack of authorial self-consciousness and philosophical maturity is the chosen form for her self-expression: the allegorization of her concerns—entrapment within a society and alienation from a true self—and the distanciation of sex and species, both of which formalize, sentimentalize, and undermine her social critique. The emphasis placed on purely animalistic or sensuous self-knowledge also clouds her vision of rebellion: the animal moves away from selfishness and towards consciousness, but that movement is one which remains limited despite Chopin's attempt to suggest the emergence of total selfhood (consciousness of mind and body rather than body split from mind). Furthermore, that the "revolt" of her brute antagonist is effected by accident romanticizes the actual process of coming to consciousness, making of it an aleatory, spontaneous leap of faith from an accepted and good enclosure to an accepted and better "Unknown" (37). Finally, and to be expected from so young a writer, such an emancipation is rewarded, and even suffering is ameliorated by the "seeking, finding, joying" (38) of the animal's continued journey through life. Chopin was clearly aware of the seductive power of nonconsciousness implicitly revealed in the protected life of a nurtured pet just as she was sympathetic to defiance. However, she was not yet able to elucidate the dialectical tension between submission and rebellion, the process of coming to consciousness that informs and is *The Awakening*. The seeds of revolt, in any case, are sown, her focus on ideological conflict begun. Having once romanticized the struggle for selfhood, Chopin would thereafter deromanticize ideological entrapment, meticulously disclosing in her later works the individual's painful journey toward true self through abysses of solitude.

Three of her earliest stories flesh out in female characters her first brutal reading of individual within and without society. All are built upon the ideology of true womanhood; yet each is strikingly dissimilar in its portrayal of woman reaching toward self-consciousness. "A No-Account Creole," first written as "Euphrasie" in 1888 and rewritten in 1890 and in January-February 1891, reveals a woman within the traditional patriarchy. "Wiser Than a God," written in June 1889, draws the world of the woman as artist. "A Point at Issue!", written in August 1889, examines the woman as divided self desirous of both self-fulfillment and union with another.

Chopin's renaming of "Euphrasie" as "A No-Account Creole" perhaps best reveals her theme and self-consciousness, in the negative sense, as a writer. Although Euphrasie is the center of the story, she is, like the animal in "Emancipation," a paragon of passivity. Despite Chopin's female allegiance, it must have seemed obvious finally both to editor and to writer that a title indicating the agent of the plot would be more acceptable to conventional, ideologically bound readers.

Euphrasie inadvertently instigates the action and conflict detailed in the story when she writes her father's New Orleans creditors about the sorry state of their plantation. She does not do so out of sheer willfulness but for the sake of duty, justice, and, perhaps, for a bit of excitement. In any case, this action takes place before the story proper begins, thus marginalizing Euphrasie's will in a curious way even though this is her story. The conflict and drama depicted relies upon, instead, the actions of Euphrasie's two men: Placide Santien, the darkly handsome, violent Creole of the second title; and Wallace Offdean, the "well-clipped and groomed," cool creditor (88). Who will win Euphrasie is the central question, and the oppositeness of the two men is the dramatic mechanism of the tale. Euphrasie is at the center of their conflict, yet she does not move nor is she particularly moved or moving as a character. A dutiful daughter, student, plantation mistress, she wishes only to become a dutiful wife. She is first affianced to Placide: it is an almost predetermined union, and he loves her. Although she is attracted to Wallace, and he to her, she is content to fulfill her obligation to Placide. In short, Euphrasie believes in the ideological precept that a woman's fate is effected by men and that first come are first served with the opportunity to determine a woman's destiny.

Indeed, Euphrasie would be taken care of well by either of these two men. Placide prepares assiduously for the moment he is to bring her to his plantation home. Wallace, in turn, promises her a better plantation when he offers his hand. She can choose, of course, only one and that one has already been named, a fact which Wallace is oblivious to until she blurts it out at his proposal. While Chopin incorporates passages on love and romance within the text, it becomes clear at this point of disclosure that Chopin's story is, finally, not about love but about honor in the abstract: not Euphrasie's sense of honor which is touched upon as being somehow tainted because she has kissed a man she does not love, not Placide's honor which would have been insulted by Wallace's behavior had Wallace acted knowingly against him, not Wallace's honor since he also has been done no willful wrong. Chopin's ostensible subject is, instead, male honor in the abstract as it is expressed through love for woman or, as Wallace tells Placide, "The way to love a woman is to think first of her happiness" (101). So, when Placide jilts Euphrasie, he proves doubly honorable: he leaves the door open for Wallace, the man who has awakened his sense of honor; and he saves Euphrasie, as she makes clear, from the sin of having to make love to the wrong man (102).

Finally, the last "action" of the story is telling. Wallace asks Euphrasie if he can return to her, and this time she says nothing. He tells her that if she does *not* speak, he will know he can return. Again, she says nothing. It is clear, then, that she is a "true" woman, one who does nothing yet all good comes to her. She is one of Chopin's few perfect Southern belles, women who would keep to their place although it mean the ruination of their souls.

It is interesting that this story takes "Emancipation" one step

further without freeing itself completely of romantic melodra-
matics. Here the door to Euphrasie's senses is opened by Wallace;
here the way for Wallace to win Euphrasie is made clear by
Placide, who does so by following Wallace's advice. In both actions, the power comes from without Euphrasie—notably, from
men. Most striking is that Euphrasie's nonconsciousness of her
own power, that over men and thus over her own fate, never
changes, never becomes even a partial consciousness but remains
marginal throughout the plot. Yet the trace of Euphrasie's power
and the fact that her passivity masks an inner torment reflect
both Chopin's own authorial passivity and desire. The reader is
made aware, even in this conventional tale, that surface does not
necessarily reveal substance: the assumption that silence equates
with acquiescence need not be true. That Chopin will later offer
detailed portrayal of the ideologically true woman who speaks
of and to her situation, notably in her characterization of Adèle
Ratignolle in *The Awakening*, suggests that even in her earliest
and seemingly most conventional fiction, Chopin was subtly subversive, if not speaking clearly her discontent or disbelief at least
murmuring the same in her submerged text.

"Wiser Than a God" presents the highly dramatic and at times
also melodramatic moment of crisis in the life of pianist Paula
Von Stoltz: she must choose between the call of art and the call
of love. Again, Chopin draws the mind/body split, this time,
however, without recourse to fabular conceit or fairy-tale ending.
Chopin will allow no conventional compromise here. It is mildly
astonishing to read Paula's refusal of George Brainard's proposal. At the same time, it is not unexpected, at the end, to see
Paula rewarded for her show of will with the admiration of
Professor Max Kuntzler, "her teacher of harmony" (44).

Chopin's revelation coupled with unconventional resolution
and conventional conclusion is that of Paula's character, the
pragmatic but determined artist. Paula is neither the dilettante
nor the starving bohemian (characterizations seen in Wharton's
similar art versus marriage stories). It is true that she stands
outside of high society because of her art: she produces on demand what George Brainard's class desires. More important,
however, is the fact that she is socially alienated because of her
class, nationality, and—by the story's middle point—her solitude.

Despite her negative background of neither wealth nor community, Paula perceives herself as a self-fulfilled and self-fulfilling individual. Since marriage to George would necessitate her response to the call of true womanhood rather than that of artist, Paula's rejection reveals her determination to support herself, albeit through temporary compromise of her full aspirations, and to produce art but not to be consumed by its buyers (a decision strikingly similar to Chopin's case). She is a woman artist who addresses her mental powers to the realization of deep desire: to speak her body through her art. In the story, she comes to understand fully the opposition between and interrelationship of illusion and reality, sentiment and emotion, desire and need. Paula then chooses to follow the purpose of her life even though she be deemed "a mad woman" (46) by George and his ilk, to position herself in a state of liminality. By the conclusion, it is clear that the narrator/author, not one of George's world, believes Paula to be wiser than a god.

Foreshadowing another important subtext in *The Awakening*, Chopin here also develops a continuum of relationships obtained between men and women by deconstructing abstract male attitudes toward women into particular types of social practices. In brief, Chopin separates men into friends or lovers, companions or husbands, stereotypes again but ones less reliant on fairy-tale romantics. Chopin also sets out different female responses to the call of womanhood: women either become wives and mothers, as George's unnamed "pretty little black-eyed fairy" (43) does, eschewing even the mundane art she appreciates; or exiles, as Paula becomes when she purposely moves to Europe. Of course, Chopin suggests that a woman might have the best of both worlds, harmony in every sense of the word, if she meets a man who could be both friend and lover, but this union of opposites is not effected within the story itself. Paula's abyss of solitude is brightened by her eventual renown and Max's presence in her life. We are not, however, led to believe that her self-exile is any less real and painful. Chopin makes clear, then, that women love, but for the salvation of their selves, they might not allow themselves to live out that love. Such will be the dilemma facing Edna Pontellier, and such will be the life choice of Mademoiselle Reisz in *The Awakening*.

In "A Point at Issue!" Chopin further complicates the theme of pure intellect in conflict with pure emotion as well as her neat bifurcation of male roles. Charles Faraday, a mathematics professor, meets student Eleanor Gail, is first physically attracted to her, and then comes to perceive her as "his ideal woman," "a logical woman" (49). In short, she shatters his ideological expectations, "an adorned picture of woman as he had known her" (49), and becomes the new woman of whom he has heretofore only dreamed. Perceiving her as his ideal equal, he would be both friend and lover, beyond ideological constraints:

Marriage was to be a form, that while fixing legally their relation to each other, was in no wise to touch the individuality of either; that was to be preserved intact. Each was to remain a free integral of humanity, responsible to no dominating exactions of so-called marriage laws. And the element that was to make possible such a union was trust in each other's love, honor, courtesy, tempered by the reserving clause of readiness to meet the consequences of reciprocal liberty. (50)

Eleanor wholly acquiesces to this, finding Charles equally ideal, although in different ways. Charles is notably conservative, is a man of reason despite his desire to make a different kind of union. He is also a secure member of his society, academia. Eleanor, on the other hand, is the true revolutionary despite her decision to be, at first, led by Charles into an "intellectual existence" (50). She is outside his established world but also determined to remain free of "public notice" (48). She is weary of compromising social proprieties and instead wishes her union to effect "the satisfying consciousness of roaming the heights of free thought, and tasting the sweets of a spiritual emancipation" (48). For her, solitude and contemplation are to be transformed into intercourse and revelation; transcendence is all. For him, the best of both worlds remains desirable. It is this incompatibility between the desires of conventional men and of radical women that ruptures their new marriage and destroys Eleanor.

Both ostensibly live up to their pact. Eleanor stays in France after their honeymoon to perfect her French; Charles returns to the university. The difference of view is immediately obvious. Eleanor progresses; Charles regresses. She surrounds herself with books and throws herself into a new world; Charles returned to his old one, "to his duties at the university, and resumed his bachelor existence as quietly as though it had been interrupted but by the interval of a day" (51). Furthermore, Eleanor continues to see them as two selves with one purpose; Charles makes them one—"She was himself" (52), thus denying their individuality. Most important, Charles returns not only to his secure, staid world, but he also begins to act and to communicate as one deeply entrenched within society. He becomes attracted to another woman and writes Eleanor of her, knowing himself that his is not a serious interest but merely social flirtation and ego-gratification. Eleanor, since she lives outside society and is unaware of Charles' reconstitution of his conservative, social self, assumes their pact has begun in earnest, that they are living an open marriage. And she follows suit. When they reunite several months later, it becomes clear that they can no longer communicate but that neither understands nor wishes to comprehend why.

Charles' true possessive nature has, by the end, come to the fore: he has not thought this out, but "he began to wonder if there might not be modifications to this marital liberty of which he was so staunch an advocate" (56). Eleanor has also surrendered her intellect to her emotions: she reveals, " 'I have been over the whole ground myself, over and over, but it is useless. I have found that there are certain things which a woman can't philosophize about, any more than she can about death when it touches that which is near to her!' " (58). Charles communes only with himself and remains deluded in the end; however, he loses neither self nor Other: " 'I love her none the less for it, but my Nellie is only a woman, after all!' " (58). Eleanor explores her self and reveals it to Charles, yet in doing so, she effaces herself and then can no longer philosophize about her own self-death: " 'I think nothing!' " (58).

Chopin here delimits the boundaries of ideology and elaborates upon the results both of traversing those boundaries and of compromising the self. She reveals a possible alternative to patriarchal convention and then how impossible, at least in this case, it is to attain. Close examination of her character development further reveals that it is the boundaries of a woman's life that are the points at issue. Charles is from beginning to end at the secure center of the societal web. Eleanor who begins almost beyond it and who attempts to reform its boundaries by her very act of living is finally brought into the center as well: she becomes not Charles, as he romanticizes, but merely his reflection, the shadow of her true self. The mind/body split seen in the first story is reenacted, but this time the mind is surrendered, the inner self lost through capitulation. Chopin here rewrites the fable and romances of her earlier work as pessimistic realism, the lightness of those tales transformed into darkness. Except in those works wherein Chopin falls back upon myths and melodrama, there will be no more simple happy endings.

At Fault, written between 5 July 1889 and 20 April 1890, marks Chopin's first full-scale attempt at controversial content expressed through conventional form. Like her earliest stories, this first novel shows her artistic and philosophical development as well as her shortcomings. *At Fault* is both unexpected revelation and partial compromise. As with any woman's work that straddles in unladylike fashion the gap between sentimental and social fiction, it is necessary to pay attention both to what Chopin explicitly says and to what she cannot or will not yet say but which she embeds in her text. To do so, one must pull apart the multiple layers of her novel to get at her core concerns.

Simply, *At Fault* is a story of problematic love. Thérèse Lafirme, a widow in her thirties, inherits her husband's Cane River plantation, Place-Du-Bois. Through a business venture, she meets David Hosmer, a northerner, and they quickly fall in love. So too do Grégoire Santien, Thérèse's nephew, a hot-blooded, overly romantic Creole (and brother of the equally hot-blooded Placide in "A No-Account Creole") and Melicent Hosmer, David's sister, an "independent" woman who lives off her brother and who is a melodramatic sap, an almost caricatural new woman. David, however, is divorced from an alcoholic, and his ex-wife Fanny still lives. Thérèse, a Catholic southerner of the old morality, cannot accept new mores and, in essence, forces David to rewed Fanny and to bring her to Cane River so that Thérèse can have David with her while they ostensibly live out her moral code by making Fanny happy. Fanny eventually succumbs to her weakness and, in a highly melodramatic climax,

drowns. Similarly, Grégoire's and Melicent's affair is destroyed
when he kills a racially-mixed firebrand who burns down David's
sawmill. That cold-blooded murder, even if of a dangerous ter-
rorist, morally disgusts Melicent, and she leaves Grégoire. Grégoire then dies violently, leaving Melicent to do a moral about-
face as she grieves for him in melodramatic fashion. Finally, as
in the best of all sentimental romances, Thérèse and David are
married and, one assumes, live happily ever after.

It should be evident from the above that Chopin's experimentation lies in her premises and not in her close. Perhaps
because she chose to focus on such a controversial issue as divorce
while she also critiqued the rise of industrial capitalism, she felt
compelled to end her various plots with convenient and seemingly conventional conclusions—in other words, to make a last
curtsy to propriety and popular taste. But just how enervating
are her textual compromises in the light of such radical content?
It is hard to deny the revisionary intent of her text, and, indeed,
the title of her work is, one might argue, consciously self-reflex-
ive. Just as the reader is led to see that everyone in the novel is
flawed in some crucial way, so too does Chopin suggest that
conventional literature and the world it depicts and glorifies are
dangerously at fault.

The few critics who have done serious study of this work tend
to bypass questions of form and to focus instead on the most
obvious yet crucially innovative level of the text: the economic
critique. Unlike many local colorists, Chopin is not intent on
painting a picture of an idyllic South. Instead, she places her
novel in the post-Reconstruction South and focuses on the
changes occurring on the land and in the industry because of
the arrival of northern capitalist methods and ethics. *At Fault*,
then, can be seen as a political and economic battleground. Furthermore, as Joyce Ruddel Ladenson writes:

The dialectic is right out of Marx: feudal power conflicts with rising
bourgeois power, with the inevitable triumph of the latter. The catch
here is that contrary to the standard class conflict which at the highest
levels takes place between men, this conflict combines class and sex, the
feudal world represented by a woman tied to an older European culture.
(32)

In this type of reading, Thérèse and David are not merely romantic or colorful individuals; more importantly, they are members of two different but now conjoined ensembles of human and economic relations. Chopin's presentation and development of characters thus complementarily offer socio-political analysis and criticism.

For example, Thérèse's world is seen, on the one hand, as built on firm and high morals, on individual sacrifice for the common good, the "sacredness of a trust" Thérèse shares with other living and dead southerners to uphold the old true way, feudal agrarianism (741). On the other hand, that Thérèse's morality is relative and, indeed, based on oppression of the common people and not always willful self-sacrifice is also shown: on her land lies the grave of McFarlane, a character based on the real-life Robert McAlpin who was, in turn, the inspiration for Stowe's Simon Legree; not all her ex-slaves or their descendants, notably the rebel Joçint, are as content as her old mammy, Marie Louise, is with their state of powerlessness in her world; more explicitly, Grégoire, her blood relative, stands as a negative exemplar of southern consciousness. Similarly, David's world is seen from opposing viewpoints. That his true world, industrial capitalism, allows new freedom for workers and women is obvious, particularly so in the case of his sister who is both a conspicuous consumer and a woman of leisure. That his system is also based on oppression and relative morality is again made clear through the actions of Joçint, the slave's son become wage slave; through description of Fanny's bourgeois, morally corrupt friends; and through his sister Melicent's own response to events, particularly her hypocritical "mourning" of her moral counterpart, Grégoire. As Lewis Leary makes clear, it is not for either world a case of absolute good or evil: "The fault may be interpreted as that of an agrarian, land-preserving South, lulled by traditions of ease and morality and religion, as it fails to respond to the industrial, land-destroying North, whose morality is modern and utilitarian. Or it may be the other way round" (178).

Chopin's acknowledgment of moral relativity and self-doubt in times of social and economic transformation is farsighted; it is her movement away from absolutes which informs her superficially romantic text and makes of it more than what it at first appears to be. Indeed, to understand fully Chopin's final political position and statement necessitates moving to another level of the text, that of the story of the individual's search for a moral, socially responsible, and self-fulfilling existence. It is also at this level of Thérèse's and David's love story that Chopin's critique of socio-sexual politics, particularly that of true womanhood ideology, implicit in the economic subtext, becomes evident.

Thérèse Lafirme is, first and foremost, a southern lady of the old tradition. She is fully complicit with womanhood ideology, so much so that she moves residence away from the newly built railroad to avoid the encroaching hordes of northern capitalist barbarians of whom David Hosmer is one. She rebuilds in the old style and, in fact, attempts to uphold single-handedly the old way of plantation life even while she capitalizes, personally and financially, on her relationship with David. Though she passes a singular year in his company, she still advocates true womanhood precepts: she reminds him continuously that she is no individualist and that she gladly effaces herself for the sake of others. Her self-martyrdom excuses her powerful position as plantation mistress: she acts as overlord merely to comply with duty and not as an expression of self-will. Similarly, once she learns of David's marital situation, she again sacrifices her own desire for the sake of another and in doing so simultaneously acts as martyr and moral guardian to David and Fanny. Thérèse thus appears to be morally and spiritually superior, sexually pure, the womanly ideal. By the novel's end, however, Chopin exposes such self-effacement as morally ambiguous (at best), socially negligent, individually destructive, and, in the case of Fanny, death-dealing.

As Thérèse's ideological counterpart, David is equally pure in his behavior. Once Thérèse tells him that he must be a man and face the consequences of his actions, he willingly accepts her as moral guide: "He felt her to be a woman with moral perceptions keener than his own and his love, which in the past twenty-four hours had grown to overwhelm him, moved him now to a blind submission" (769). Though he is in "anguish of spirit" (770), he returns to Fanny, remarries her, and attempts to live up to Thérèse's standards for him. He continues to do so even after

he realizes he hates Fanny, even after he moves Fanny to Place-
Du-Bois and must then see both women each day, even after
Fanny descends into alcoholic schizophrenia again. By the nov-
el's end, Chopin makes clear once more that such self-martyr-
dom is not only repressive but also hypocritical and, again for
Fanny, lethal.

It is through the disturbed character of Fanny that Chopin
disorders the neat sexual and moral hierarchies at the base of
womanhood ideology and of her text. One can read Fanny as
pure stereotype: Fanny as the fallen woman. Chopin makes her
more than that by offering in a minimum of words Fanny's side
of the story. She is a woman fallen into alienation, a true woman
in that she is powerless and self-less. Through Fanny's eyes, the
reader sees another David, as real a man as Thérèse's lover, and
learns why after the first marriage Fanny "began to dread him
and defy him" (779). David's relationship with Fanny had been
superficial from the start. David had quickly labelled her as beneath him in class, and Fanny had just as quickly "felt herself
as of little consequence, and in a manner, overlooked" (798).
Her desire and self-will are deemed unimportant, especially after
the death of their only child, a son; she is at most David's helpmeet and, during the second marriage, treated as *his* child. In
essence, David, following Thérèse's will, drives Fanny to desperate means and to her eventual despairing end. For example,
after their reunion and despite his knowledge of her "sensitivity,"
he uproots Fanny from her secure if morally tainted world and
forces her move to an alien and alienating land. It is not surprising, then, that on her first night in Thérèse's world Fanny
finds "a certain mistrust was creeping into her heart with the
nearing darkness" (794). The coming of night suggests not only
the mental darkness of Fanny's stupors; it also foreshadows Fanny's end as well as recognition of the truth of her existence and
perceptions: the moral murkiness of her marriage, the rude
erasure of her hope when she later hears David who becomes
at one point deliriously ill call Thérèse's name instead of her
own and who later threatens to kill her if she take Thérèse's
name in vain, the moral and spiritual blindness she faces as she
realizes that neither David nor Thérèse acknowledges her desire,

the irreparable loss of herself in her constant position of oth-
erness, the final inky darkness that is her death.

The destruction of Fanny's precariously maintained sense of
self because of the moral theories and practices of Thérèse and
David judges darkly both womanhood ideology and the patriarchal, whether feudal or capitalist. If an individual, even if only a
weak woman, can be driven into solitude and alienation by accepted morality for her own good, what then is the difference between morality and immorality? Similarly, if a man sacrifices his
life only to destroy another's, what is the social value of such self-
effacement? Finally, if a woman were to realize the cost of womanhood morality and that there is not one true, faultless way of
being, how then does she or anyone live? Chopin's answer to the
last is the "moral" of her tale: some women and men do not survive; some do, but only after questioning authority, admitting
self-will, and accepting self-doubt and continual self-transfor-
mation as the basis of existence in an, at best, amoral world.

Chopin suggests such a survivor in the character counterpart
to Fanny: Homeyer, the man closest to David. Homeyer's philosophy of life and reaction to David's actions are continually
recalled by David at crucial moments. For instance, David reviews
Homeyer's response to his remarriage and the moral issues involved:

And what had Homeyer said of it? He had railed of course as usual,
at the submission of a human destiny to the exacting and ignorant rule
of what he termed moral conventionalities. He had startled and angered
Hosmer with his denunciation of Thérèse's sophistical guidance.
Rather—he proposed—let Hosmer and Thérèse marry, and if Fanny
were to be redeemed—though he pooh-poohed the notion as untenable
with certain views of what he called the rights to existence: the existence
of wrongs—sorrows—diseases—death—let them all go to make up the
conglomerate whole—and let the individual man hold on to his personality. But if she must be redeemed—granting this point to their
littleness, let the redemption come by different ways than those of
sacrifice: let it be an outcome from the capability of their united happiness. (777)

David, the slave to "Love's prophet," Thérèse, cannot at this
point in the story accept Homeyer's advice, but neither can he

totally cast it from his mind (777). Later, David recalls another
conversation concerning religions, applicable to Thérèse's Ca-
tholicism, and social evolution, ideas unheard of in his and
Thérèse's philosophy:

"Homeyer would have me think that all religions are but mythological
creations invented to satisfy a species of sentimentality—a morbid craving in man for the unknown and undemonstrable. . . . he believes in a
natural adjustment . . . In an innate reserve force of accommodation.
What we commonly call laws in nature, he styles accidents—in society,
only arbitrary methods of expediency, which, when they outlive their
usefulness to an advancing and exacting civilization, should be set aside.
He is a little impatient to always wait for the inevitable natural adjustment." (792–793)

Homeyer, then, is a man beyond the manners and morals of
David and Thérèse, a sophisticated realist coupling a long-range
optimism with immediate pessimism. Homeyer is also a character
beyond the text: he neither appears, nor is he given a verifiable
existence. Homeyer is such an illusory and visionary being, in
fact, that Thérèse early on surmises he is David's alter-ego. Chopin never corroborates this interpretation in her narration but
instead leaves Homeyer a voice deeply embedded in David and
strangely distanced within the text. However, just as Thérèse
speculates that Homeyer is David's inner voice, it is textual coun-
terpoint to conjecture that Homeyer is the text's other narrator,
Chopin's secret critical voice. This theory is given substance by
Thérèse's awakening to new consciousness and by the lovers'
final discourse.

Thérèse begins to question her moral allegiance and purposes
once Fanny arrives at Place-Du-Bois. She hears Fanny's story
and thereafter sees before her the effects of her moral stance.
Her self-sacrifice is shown to be futile and selfish; her morals
become less self-glorifying: she thinks, "Were Fanny, and her
own prejudices, worth the sacrifice which she and Hosmer had
made?" (808) Later she ponders whether her morality is finally
a nurturance or a denial of life: "the doubt assailed her whether
it were after all worth while to strive against the sorrows of life
that can be so readily put aside" (810). At the same time David
comes to realize that their morality costs too much but that he

cannot break faith with Thérèse. At this point, however, it clearly becomes solely Thérèse's duty to offer moral support to both of them since it was her will that their lives be so and it is now only within her power to make those lives bearable. Shortly thereafter, Thérèse dreams that her actions to save David had only served to kill him. She here subconsciously recognizes the relativity of her morality:

She had always thought this lesson of right and wrong a very plain one. So easy of interpretation that the simplest minded might solve it if they would. And here had come for the first time in her life a staggering doubt as to its nature. . . . She continued to ask herself only "was I right?" and it was by the answer to that question that she would abide, whether in the stony content of accomplished righteousness, or in an enduring remorse that pointed to a goal in whose labyrinthine possibilities her soul lost itself and fainted away. (840)

But there are no easy either-or answers available to Thérèse, and she consciously enters a state of contemplation and self-doubt. Grégoire's death, as well as Joçint's murder, makes righteousness impossible: Grégoire is of her blood, and she therefore believes that she shares responsibility for all the bloodshed. She accepts then that the ideology which she has advocated has proven to be at least partially based on immorality and hypocrisy. Her relationship with David and Fanny serves to foreground this realization. As she tells David after Fanny's death, " 'I have seen myself at fault in following what seemed the only right. I feel as if there were no way to turn for the truth. Old supports appear to be giving way beneath me. They were so secure before' " (872). And so Thérèse precariously balances between self-recrimination and self-loss.

David offers Thérèse and himself a way out but not, as one would expect of a less complicated work, by offering his new supports—bourgeois ethics—as alternative world view. David has also seen into the heart of his morality which is, obviously, not that dissimilar from Thérèse's. For all their seemingly crucial differences—sex, class, mores—David and Thérèse are still identically caught in the deadly web of hegemonic ideology, and, as David points out, it is not within those traditional boundaries that they will acquire self-knowledge:

"Thérèse," said Hosmer firmly, "the truth in its entirety isn't given to man to know—such knowledge, no doubt, would be beyond human endurance. But we make a step towards it, when we learn that there is rottenness and evil in the world, masquerading as right and morality— when we learn to know the living spirit from the dead letter. I have not cared to stop in this struggle of life to question. You, perhaps, wouldn't dare to alone. Together, dear one, we will work it out. Be sure there is a way—we may not find it in the end, but we will at least have tried." (872)

It is a declaration such as Homeyer might have made.

The novel's conclusion reestablishes difference and offers a quick glimpse at transcendence of separation. David and Thérèse marry and begin a new life which incorporates the best of their old worlds but which is beyond the strictures and norms of the traditional. David while still the sensible capitalist has learned sensitivity through his experience with Thérèse. Similarly, Thérèse while yet the plantation mistress is no longer a firm frozen saint but has instead come to acknowledge and to express her individual desire. The joining of old and new worlds, the marriage of land and industry, of South and North, of woman and man result finally in a utopic union of promising and profitable love. Chopin, however, does not descend into sentimental romance here. She makes clear that transcendence coupled with self-fulfillment is possible but that the potentiality lies solely within the power and will of each individual: the reader is not privy to David's and Thérèse's last whispered words. Self-fulfillment is not presented as a finished product, a commodity that one can purchase cheaply, but as a process one must effect. Chopin only indicates that some words of desire and will can be said and heard by those who refuse self-effacement, those who continually strive to understand the "living spirit"; but these words cannot be inscribed in traditional texts, cannot be spelled out in "dead letter." The conclusion of *At Fault*—unlike the dead ending of "A Point at Issue!"—is open-ended "natural adjustment" and offers not so much a resolution as a glimpse of a new world, one of unspeakable delight.

The partial compromise of the text lies in the forms and techniques Chopin uses. Chopin was not yet such a sufficiently sophisticated writer and social critic to be able to produce a completely unified work of social fiction. Too often her central concerns play second role to stereotypical characterization, witty stabs at minor issues, and her expert but disruptive introduction of dialect. The melodramatic Grégoire-Melicent love story does not finally add as much as it distracts from the development of the realistic main plot and the ethical issues therein. The conflation of fate and self-will is also heavy-handed since it is abruptly and violently forced as climax. Most problematic is Chopin's use of Black characters. Thérèse's lived experience is predicated upon the use of Blacks as labor power, as constituents of the feudal slave culture with which she is first identified. One of the most disturbing elements of the novel is that Black characters must die, in essence be sacrificed, so that she may relinquish her sense of totality to the new ideology embodied in David; one may look to Helen Taylor's critique of *At Fault* for a fuller account of this problem. *At Fault* was, of course, Chopin's first novel, and in several sections it reads as such.

That Chopin herself felt the inadequacy of her novelistic skills can be intuited from her return to the short story form. She seemed to comprehend that her own critical impatience with large-scale plot manipulation made her resort to textual methods of expediency in order to foreground her philosophical end statements, that she had attempted too much too soon. She might, as well, also have been discouraged by the reception accorded her first novel. Whatever the case, she turned back to short fiction and used it once more as a testing ground for the themes, images, and techniques introduced here and later brought together so well in her final masterpiece, *The Awakening*. She continued to call attention to the process of coming to consciousness, a critical process only partially realized and elaborated in *At Fault*.

Though Kate Chopin would continue to experiment with various fictional forms, her post–1891 work focuses more and more on the oppressiveness of womanhood ideology and the arduousness of woman's quest for self. This development is particularly striking when one considers the popularity of Chopin's less adventurous work, her local color stories. That Chopin had more to say than what could be said through conventional fiction is patent; that she had the courage to do so, risking the loss of reputation and audience, is both strange and rare.

One cannot know what made Chopin follow the literary course she did. One can speculate that after the total rejection of her second novel, *Young Dr. Gosse*, begun almost immediately after *At Fault* and finished in November 1890, she realized what was acceptable and what was not. One can go further, however, and theorize that her post–1891 stories reveal that she chose nonetheless to make central in her fiction that which was not to be written or said in genteel literature. The increasingly revisionary subject matter on which her mid-career stories depend suggests that Chopin wished both to subvert and to challenge true womanhood ideology in her work and that she was herself progressively informed by the critical process she persistently pursued despite censure. Her major stories of this period can be categorized as addressing three themes under the heading of ideology: the solitary awakening of the alienated individual, the virtues and failings of motherhood as a means to self-fulfillment, and the realm of the senses as the battleground for the self.

Her 1891 stories for the most part break no new ground and read as fairly conventional historical and local color tales. Her main energy was then going toward the promotion of her two novels. There are, to be sure, unconventional heroines even here: Marianne in "The Maid of Saint Phillippe" (written 19 April 1891), Fifine in "A Very Fine Fiddle" (13 September 1891), Boulotte in "Boulôt and Boulotte" (20 September 1891), Lolotte Bordon in "A Rude Awakening" (13 July 1891). All are social exiles because of class or circumstance; except for the mythic Marianne, all are pragmatic survivors who break convention for good reason and thus are finally not such rebellious figures as may appear so on first reading. Less easily rationalized are those stories in which Chopin purposely focuses on alienation; these works rise above the ordinary, though not all do so to the same degree. Two of her earliest stories in this vein, "Beyond the Bayou" (7 November 1891) and "After the Winter" (31 December 1891), fail to show the roots of social conflict that effect an alienated life. In both, the protagonists, the African-American La Folle and the ruined southerner Michel, have been driven

insane by their experiences of war and its atrocities. Both reject
society until, by accident, they are brought back into the fold
through the acts of children. Chopin does not investigate the
causes of self-exile in these particular cases, nor does she seem
to desire anything less than full reconciliation of individual with
society. There is a hint, however, that society has changed its
ways at least partially because of the actions of its self-exiled; in
both stories, society waits with open arms for the return of its
critics, and it is a warm world of "infinite peace" and childlike
innocence (188). At the same time, it is a radiant world only at
its center; as Michel perceives, even in his transcendent moment,
there is always "the hill far off that was in black shadow against
the sky" (188). Chopin hereafter concerns herself almost obsessively with the black shadows on the social margins. In this line
of her work, she is no longer content with emancipation from
alienation if it only leads to return to the old world that is still
bordered in darkness.

"Ma'ame Pélagie," written 27–28 August 1892, and "Désirée's
Baby," written 24 November 1892, clearly mark her break with
traditional reconciliation themes and superficially happy endings. In both, she takes up the true woman paradigm, sets it in
the historical contexts of an antebellum and a postbellum South,
and subtly exposes the destructive will-to-power which relies
upon womanhood ideology for its realization.

"Désirée's Baby" takes place in the old South, and the reader
is presented with two portraits of that time and place. One centers on the genteel and peaceful Valmondé, grand plantation of
a couple of the same name. Here Désirée is abandoned as a baby
and taken up as the Valmondés' own child. At the outset of the
story, she is eighteen, has grown "to be beautiful and gentle,
affectionate and sincere,—the idol of Valmondé" (240). She has
just left her perfect world for L'Abri, the plantation of her impassioned husband, Armand Aubigny.

L'Abri is the black horizon glimpsed in Chopin's earlier story.
Unlike Valmondé, it is a dark world of sadness and barely restrained brutality. The passions of its master result not in love
and fruitfulness for this world, as they do at first for Désirée,
but in ruthlessness and sterility. It is a world of power in which
Armand's will and desire color everything, just as the oaks

around his house "shadowed it like a pall" (241). Désirée's conflicting emotions of happiness and fear felt early on in their marriage (242) foreshadow their fall into individual darkness and despair. It comes as no surprise at the end that the one symbol of a bright new world, Désirée's newborn son, should prove death-dealing precisely because it has been darkened, both figuratively and literally, by Armand.

Once it becomes evident that their son is a mulatto, Désirée loses everything: Armand throws her from the pedestal on which he had placed her down to the lowest level of animal, though Chopin immediately clarifies for the reader that it is Armand who is the inhuman beast and not Désirée (243). The checked cruelty of Armand, reined in after his marriage, is unleashed: the slaves suffer as does their supposed sister, Désirée, and it is all her fault. That Désirée is blamed for the impurity of their son is both circumstantial and telling. Monsieur Valmondé had foreseen such a situation before the wedding, stressing the uncertainty of her parentage. Armand had responded to his warnings about her obscure past by saying that the Aubigny name would make Désirée into the compleat ideal. Here Chopin reveals the base of true womanhood, male power, and the agency of feminine self-fulfillment, male desire. Even though Armand himself has a somewhat shadowy past and an equally dark present, there is never a moment, until the final disclosure, that suspicion falls on anyone but Désirée. In this way Chopin utilizes the theme of racism to illuminate her critical reading of woman's extreme vulnerability if she chooses to live according to patriarchal prescriptives. Chopin drives home the truth that no matter how such a woman might live, no matter what she might make herself to be, she can be destroyed, and with full social sanction, if she does not fit the specified model in every particular way, even in those ways outside her control. In Armand's world, Désirée deserves social oblivion or death since she has passed herself off as other than what she should have been: her reality, rooted in her body, is a black stain on him and his world, "upon his home and his name" (244).

Désirée also comes to believe herself doomed, though not at fault. Ever a true woman, she remains oblivious to the very last of her rights and her nascent power as well as profoundly limited in her consciousness, both of her situation and of herself. She is the last to realize her child is black; she is the last to acquiesce to the "fact" that she must be the cause of this since her husband has said it is so. However, she also never accepts her fall from true womanhood, and this is what finally destroys her. Her identity is inextricably dependent upon her relationship to Armand as his wife and mother of his child. If he denies his child and no longer desires her, Désirée is not only abandoned, but she is no longer Désirée; as Peggy Skaggs argues in *Kate Chopin*, "her place and even her name depend upon man's regarding her as a prized possession" (26). Schooled too well in the manners and constraints of true womanhood, Désirée herself denies the possibility of life outside Armand's world and instead chooses a suicidal descent into and not beyond the bayou. Even though Chopin makes clear at the end that Désirée was not "at fault"— Armand's mother was racially mixed—Chopin also indicates that her exoneration is not the point at issue but that her self-destruction is: Anna Shannon Elfenbein points out, "It does not really matter whether she is white or black, since her very life depends on the whims, social class, and race of her husband" (127). Her "total powerlessness" is "the result of the life-and-death power of the husband in her society" (131).

Chopin does suggest ways of escape for women. One is the path chosen by Armand's mother, again a woman whose life was dependent on male compassion and power. The father proves more humane than the son, but this does not compensate for the mother's life of exile and her burial in an alien land. Another way is offered by Madame Valmondé. Though she accepts the "fact" of Désirée's race, she does not deny Désirée's personhood. After Désirée writes her for self-confirmation and solace, Madame Valmondé answers: " 'My own Désirée: Come home to Valmondé; back to your mother who loves you. Come with your child' " (243). She does not verify Désirée's whiteness because she cannot; she does not deny Désirée's relationship to her because she chooses not to do so. She is the character with the most liberated consciousness, then, a woman who would transcend racist and sexist ideology to protect her own, in this case the female. Désirée, of course, does not even perceive the possibility of a female world; unlike her mother, she proves to have less consciousness of her innate self. She had identified herself, as Armand did, as an idol, and like all idols is "silent, white, motionless" (243), non-conscious, easy to destroy. Once accused and abandoned, once marked as an undesirable, she cannot, as she tells her mother, survive: " 'I shall die. I must die. I cannot be so unhappy, and live' " (243). And, as in *At Fault,* Chopin leaves the reader with an awareness of where the fault for this lies: not merely in the frail hands of powerless individuals but in the actions of all individuals who support this patriarchal, racist world the social faults of which finally widen into the black abyss that engorges Désirée.

"Ma'ame Pélagie" more openly points to the ruin effected by adherence to such reactionary ideology. The story is set in a postbellum South and portrays two sisters caught between the old and new worlds seen in *At Fault.* Pélagie and Pauline Valmêt, respectively fifty and thirty-five years old, live in a comfortless log cabin beside the ruins of their mansion which was torched during the Civil War. Pélagie's only desire is to rebuild the mansion and to die there. Their niece La Petite comes to visit and despite her love of life tries to fit into their backward looking existence, finally rebelling against living solely in the past. Pauline, who has come to love La Petite, tells her sister she will die if the niece leaves since there will then be no present or future for Pauline on the Côte Joyeuse. The conflict is thus seen to be that between two worlds, both embodied within and reflected through women: the old true womanhood reality of Pélagie versus the new life, "the pungent atmosphere of an outside and dimly known world," which La Petite introduces to her and which is desired by Pauline (233). Unlike that in "Désirée's Baby," the battle here is simple and the outcome almost a given; however, the final resolution for Pélagie is a striking parallel to Désirée's last walk away from the old world.

Pélagie is the embodiment of the true southern woman, though she is not by any means the frail flower of womanhood. Despite the loss of home, wealth, and power, she clings tenaciously to the past and the dream of what once was. Even though she eventually perceives the falseness of her dream, the basic corruptness of that world view, she never renounces her past or her true womanhood conception of self as queen and martyr. She remains imperious and self-alienated to the end.

From the outset of the story, it is also clear that Pélagie is an extremely willful woman blind to her own selfishness. She has effectively ruled and ruined her sister's life for thirty years in her attempt to train her to be "a true Valmêt" (233). She forces her sister to efface herself for the sake of Pélagie's passionate goal: to reconstitute daily her own past, one that Pauline does not share since she cannot remember it. That past seductively offers a place of privilege for Pélagie, if not for her sister, one through which she would be socially secure, part of a whole that serves as a collective only in that it shelters each individual from accusation and consciousness of fault. Like Thérèse in *At Fault*, Pélagie thinks the old way is the only way and that remuneration for her own loss sanctions the forcing of her will on others.

Pélagie's denial of present reality is strong even in the face of La Petite, the girl from the world outside. In one of their first embraces, Pélagie looks only for "a likeness of the past in the living present" (234), refusing to see anything other than her dream. She is similarly untouched when her niece later grieves that life at Côte Joyeuse is killing them and when she argues against the necessity of such self-entrapment:

"it is as though a weight were pressing me backward here. I must live another life; the life I lived before. I want to know things that are happening from day to day over the world, and hear them talked about. I want my music, my books, my companions. If I had known no other life but this one of privation, I suppose it would be different. If I had to live this life, I should make the best of it. But I do not have to; and you know, tante Pélagie, you do not need to. It seems to me," she added in a whisper, "that it is a sin against myself." (234–235)

For Pélagie, La Petite is easily discounted as a new woman; she is not a true Valmêt. La Petite thinks of herself instead of Pélagie's imaginary collective, and it is of no consequence to Pélagie that that community is nearly dead. In stark contrast, Pauline sees her niece as her " 'saviour; like one who had come and taken me by the hand and was leading me somewhere—somewhere I want to go' " (235). This response suggests that she has been a hostage to her sister's territorial imperative; she has been made to live in a world not her own. It is only when Pauline says that she will die if La Petite is forced to leave because of Pélagie's morbidity that Pélagie's dream and world fall apart. Pauline is the last but for Pélagie, and she is also Pélagie's charge, for whom she believes she has always sacrificed herself. Once Pauline rejects her sister's dream world, Pélagie has no one to reflect her self-constitution, no one with whom she can dramatize herself. Yet once Pélagie has been called upon to make the ultimate sacrifice, to give up her dream for someone who no longer loves her in the old way, as a true woman she does so and in that way is obviously similar to Désirée. However, unlike Désirée, Pélagie is finally revealed to be a perversely dark womanhood exemplar, for in her final act of self-effacement, she defies all comprehension.

As was suggested earlier, Chopin portrays Pélagie throughout as a harsh and narrow-minded woman. Despite her calculated appearance as a concerned and self-sacrificing sister, Pélagie is continually exposed as an unmoved and self-seeking tyrant. She is thus also similar to Armand, both bound to concepts of honor and loyalty that deny individual desire or being beyond their own. It is after her scene with Pauline that the reader sees the true Pélagie: a living ghost whose reality lies not in this world but in the ruined and ruinous past. She walks through the destroyed mansion, oblivious to actual "light or dark" (236), "to see the visions that hitherto had crowded her days and nights, and to bid them farewell" (236). She relives her past, her initial denial of war threats, her romanticized memories of the slaves' lot. Even as she recalls the slaves' revolt, she embraces nonconsciousness, complicit denial of the knowledge that her world could be built on violence and oppression. Abruptly, she feels again her desire to kill a Black woman, then to die in the fire "to show them how a daughter of Louisiana can perish before her conquerors" (237). Her visions are both grotesquely cruel and wildly sentimental, and her dream is revealed as a superficial whitewashing of the actual nightmare past. The reader also sees that Pélagie's reactionary and racist nonconsciousness constitutes her past and her relation to life, that it is actually Pauline, and not her dream, that has made her live on precisely because Pauline, like the Black woman, has never fit into Pélagie's vision of self and world. Pauline once kept her from the perfect heroine's death; Pauline, no matter what now occurs, will thus always keep her from recapturing the past potential of self-perfectability. Yet Pélagie is a survivor, and she ultimately finds a new use for Pauline. Pauline will be the recipient of Pélagie's greatest gift. Pélagie will give her Côte Joyeuse to refashion into her own new world; she will give up her dream and herself for her sister. Pélagie thus creates an almost equally romantic and repressive vision of total self-martyrdom with which to replace her primal dream. She chooses to live alienated and alienating to the very last.

At the end, the land lives up to its name: a new house stands on the site of the ruins, one filled with pleasant companions and music. Pauline is reborn as an independent woman, and La Petite no longer need deny her true self. However, like the shadows of L'Abri, Pélagie stands alone, draped in black, just on the edge of this new world. As Chopin concludes, "How could it be different! While the outward pressure of a young and joyous existence had forced her footsteps into the light, her soul had stayed in the shadow of the ruin" (239). Unlike Madame Valmondé, Pélagie cannot transcend her social prejudices, ideological upbringing, and her limited consciousness of self in relation to others. Chopin presents nothing positive in Pélagie's past, present, or future. Furthermore, at the end Pélagie is seen to have aged suddenly as if she has been denied sustenance, perhaps an allusion to her vampiric living off the past and those who made her past possible. It is Pauline and her reality that will live, just as Thérèse does in At Fault within her new world at the end; it is a time and place of unknowns, but it is at least of "the living spirit." More important, that the new world is born through the influence of a new woman, small but sure of self, is indicative of Chopin's belief in the positive effects of some women's own will-to-power if that reflects defiance against the old ways and leads to self-realization rather than self-effacement.

Chopin had earlier written another story, "Miss McEnders" (7 March 1892), on this theme of moral guardianship and blind social consciousness, and would continue to explore this topic in later pieces. Woman's complicity with corrupt social systems and totalizing ideologies would also remain a central subject throughout Chopin's career. So too would Chopin continually return to the dilemma of desire versus duty, self-realization versus socially sanctioned self-sacrifice. She does so in such stories as "La Belle Zoraïde" (21 September 1893) and "Lilacs" (14–16 May 1894). Her most complex stories, however, take up the secondary characters introduced in the works discussed above: the Paulines, the Madame Valmondés, the women who experience some sort of personal and social awakening. In these works, Chopin offers concentrated descriptions of moments that shatter social complacency, that quickening of consciousness which gives birth to self-desire, self-recognition, and, in Chopin's fictive world, consequent despair and self-alienation. Chopin's "The Story of an Hour," written 19 April 1894, is undoubtedly her most famous and intense reading in this line.

Before discussing that story and those that follow and clearly point to *The Awakening*, one should note that Chopin first penned another portrait of a highly unconventional woman. Her development as a writer can be marked by these singular pieces: "Wiser Than a God," coming at the beginning of her career; "Azélie" written on 22–23 July 1893, both closing off the second stage and introducing the pre-*Awakening* stories; "An Egyptian Cigarette" written in April 1897 just before she began *The Awakening*; and "The Storm" written 19 July 1898 soon after she had finished her masterpiece. One could argue that each story acts as Chopin's release from the pessimistic vision developing in her work; each piece centers on a strong woman who is virtually untouched by the despair found in Chopin's more realistic fiction.

"Azélie" is conspicuously unlike Chopin's other work, a rustic fable with an almost feminist but also extremely subtle moral. Azélie is a poor farmer's daughter who neither acts nor thinks at all like Chopin's conventional women: she is a seemingly amoral, nearly Amazonian female who barely acknowledges male reality or desire. She first offends the shop-tender 'Polyte when she refuses to act according to his ideological expectations: "There was no trace of any intention of coquetry in her manner. He resented this as a token of indifference toward his sex, and thought it inexcusable" (291). Later she further disorders his physical world and his ideological world view when she breaks into his store and takes what she and her father need: "She seemed to have no shame or regret for what she had done, and plainly did not realize that it was a disgraceful act. 'Polyte often shuddered with disgust to discern in her a being so wholly devoid of moral sense" (295). Despite this assault on his masculinity and morals, he falls in love with her, primarily because he misreads her actions and presentation of self as those of a helpless damsel in distress who needs a knight in shining armor to tame and protect her:

He would keep her with him when the others went away. He longed to rescue her from what he felt to be the demoralizing influences of her family and her surroundings. 'Polyte believed he would be able to awaken Azélie to finer, better impulses when he should have her apart to himself. (296)

These romantic and ideologically conventional notions are given short shrift by Azélie, who cooly dismisses his advances: "She was not indignant; she was not flustered or agitated, as might have been a susceptible, coquettish girl; she was only astonished, and annoyed" (295). Refusing his proposal and, thus, entrance into his world, she suddenly leaves with her family for warmer climes. She is throughout her relationship with him untouched and untouchable. Though the reader is offered little insight into Azélie's personal sense of self and world, it is obvious that she, like Paula in "Wiser Than a God," chooses to position herself outside society and is content to remain there. She is alien to 'Polyte's class, undesiring of his offers of love and redemptive salvation, and, unlike Paula, she is firmly attached to and responsible toward her small community. In fact, she is so strong in will and self-constitution that her power finally draws 'Polyte away from his world at the end as he quits his store to follow in her footsteps.

Chopin perhaps suggests in this open ending that despite appearances and expectations, the alienate may lead a desirable, even enviable, existence based on responsible and responsive affection and concern. But, of course, Azélie is forever a social anomaly, like the animal in "Emancipation." Her particular case implicitly critiques conventional morality, but it does not offer an explicit model for new consciousness. Hers is a complete, self-

contained, self-sufficient world; yet her very act of living changes
the world around her, and one senses that all good things will
come to her in the end. This is not the typical condition explored
in Chopin's fiction.

"The Story of an Hour," for instance, details a very ordinary
reality and conscientiously analyzes that moment in a woman's
life when the boundaries of the accepted everyday world are
suddenly shattered and the process of self-consciousness begins.
Louise Mallard, dutiful wife and true woman, is gently told that
her husband has been killed in a train accident. Her response
is atypical, however, and that is the subject of the story: what
Louise thinks and feels as she finds herself thrust into solitude
and self-contemplation for the first time.

Louise appears in the opening as the frail, genteel, devoted
wife of a prosperous businessman; she is at first only named as
such: Mrs. Mallard. However, her first response to the tragedy
indicates a second Louise nestling within that social shell: "she
did not hear the story as many women have heard the same,
with a paralyzed inability to accept its significance. She wept at
once, with sudden, wild abandonment, in her sister's arms" (352).
Chopin thus implies that perhaps some part of Louise readily
accepts the news. She also intimates that since Louise unconsciously chooses to enfold herself in a female embrace and not
in the arms of the male friend who tells her of Mallard's death,
Louise has already turned to a female world, one in which she
is central. It is in the mid-section of the story, set in Louise's
room, that Louise and Chopin's reader explore and come to
understand reaction and potential action, social self—Mrs. Mallard—and private, female self—Louise.

Louise sits before an open window at first thinking nothing
but merely letting impressions of the outer and inner worlds
wash over her. She is physically and spiritually depleted but is
still sensuously receptive. She sees the "new spring life" (352) in
budding trees, smells rain, hears human and animal songs as
well as a man "crying his wares" (352). She is like both a tired
child dreaming a sad dream (353) and a young woman self-
restrained but with hidden strengths. She is yet Mrs. Mallard.

As she sits in "a suspension of intelligent thought" (353), she
feels something unnameable coming to her through her senses.

It is frightening because it is not of her true womanhood world; it reaches to her from the larger world outside and would "possess her" (353). The unnameable is, of course, her self-consciousness that is embraced once she names her experience as emancipation and not destitution: "She said it over and over under her breath: 'free, free, free!'... Her pulses beat fast, and the coursing blood warmed and relaxed every inch of her body" (353). It is at this point that she begins to think, the point at which she is reborn through and in her body, an experience analogous to that of Edna Pontellier in *The Awakening*.

Louise then immediately recognizes her two selves and comprehends how each will co-exist, the old finally giving way to the one new self. Mrs. Mallard will grieve for the husband who had loved her, but Louise will eventually revel in the "monstrous joy" (353) of self-fulfillment, beyond ideological strictures and the repressive effects of love:

> she would live for herself. There would be no powerful will bending hers in that blind persistence with which men and women believe they have a right to impose a private will upon a fellow-creature. A kind intention or a cruel intention made the act seem no less a crime as she looked upon it in that brief moment of illumination.
>
> And yet she had loved him—sometimes. Often she had not. What did it matter! What could love, the unsolved mystery, count for in face of this possession of self-assertion which she suddenly recognized as the strongest impulse of her being! (353)

It is only after Louise embraces this new consciousness, her sense of personal and spiritual freedom in a new world, that she is named as female self by her sister. This is no doubt ironic since her sister only unconsciously recognizes her; she can have little idea of the revolution that has taken place in Louise's own room. Yet Chopin does not allow simple utopian endings, and Louise's sister's intrusion into Louise's world also prefigures the abrupt end to her "drinking in a very elixir of life through that open window" (354).

Louise leaves her room and descends again into her past world. Though she carries herself "like a goddess of Victory" (354) and has transcended the boundaries of her past self, she is not armed for the lethal intrusion of the past world through her front door.

Brently Mallard unlocks his door and enters unharmed. His return from the dead kills Louise, and Chopin's conclusion is the critical and caustic remark that all believed "she had died of heart disease—of joy that kills" (354).

It is easy for the reader to be overwhelmed by the pathos of the story, a natural response since the reader comes to consciousness of the text just as Louise awakens to self-consciousness. Chopin offers the reader only that one point of identification—Louise, whose powers of reflection have been repressed, suddenly shocked into being, and then brutally cut off. It is a disorienting reading experience to be cut off as well after being awakened to Louise's new self-possibilities. It is also beyond irony to be left at the conclusion with the knowledge that only Louise and the reader perceived the earlier "death" of the true woman Mrs. Mallard; and that what murdered her was, indeed, a monstrous joy, the birth of individual self, and the erasure of that joy when her husband and, necessarily, her old self returned. Far from being a melodramatic ending, the conclusion both informs and warns: should a woman see the real world and her individual self within it only to be denied the right to live out that vision, then in her way lies non-sense, self-division, and dissolution. Chopin's analysis of womanhood ideology and quest for self here takes on a darker hue. Her earlier stories examined the destruction of women who lived within traditional society; this piece offers no escape for those who live outside that world but who do so only in a private world in themselves. Either way, Chopin seems to be saying, there lies self-oblivion if only the individual changes and not the world.

—At this time, Chopin also explored motherhood in several stories, no doubt as part of her own process of coming to consciousness. Louise was alone and had no other acceptable world—as ideology had pictured the world of mothers and children—in which to fulfill herself. In such works as "Regret," written 17 September 1894, and "Athénaïse," written 10–28 April 1895, Chopin depicts the female strength granted to mothers. Athénaïse, for example, is transformed by her pregnancy, which is described as both her self-contained experience and her sensuous awakening which leads to her reunion with her husband. However, as Peggy Skaggs points out in *Kate Chopin*, Ath-

énaïse pays a price for attaining wifehood and motherhood: "She
has sacrificed her name and more; she has sacrificed also her
autonomy, her right to live as a discrete individual. Athénaïse
Miché exists no longer" (38). Further, as Patricia Hopkins Lattin
argues, Athénaïse's positive experience of pregnancy is qualified
by several other motherhood stories, those in which women give
birth or have given birth. One such representation of motherhood as yet another form of ideological entrapment that some
women accept, along with the loss of self, and some do not is
"A Pair of Silk Stockings," written in April 1896. The story shows
the dark side of motherhood and builds on the major elements
from "The Story of an Hour," with only a few shifts in class and
setting. ➡

In this piece, a genteel but poor woman, seemingly without
support and alone except for her children, experiences an awakening of sensuous self. Mrs. Sommers is a woman born to a
better class than the one she married into, but she is also a true
woman who neither shirks sacrifice for her family nor thinks of
anything beyond her immediate life as mother and martyr: "She
had no time—no second of time to devote to the past. The needs
of the present absorbed her every faculty. A vision of the future
like some dim, gaunt monster sometimes appalled her, but luckily to-morrow never comes" (500–501). As in "The Story of an
Hour," the unexpected occurs: Mrs. Sommers comes into a veritable fortune, fifteen dollars, which she at first plans to spend
on her children. Like Louise Mallard, she is physically and spiritually exhausted when she arrives at the moment of contemplation and action. One begins to see more clearly Chopin's
definition of the usual effect of womanhood ideology: self-
depletion. Again just like Louise, she experiences a sensuous
moment—here the particularly female response to a specifically
feminine luxury, silk stockings—which reawakens her female
self, an experience which simultaneously embraces her and engulfs her in monstrous joy from which there is no desire for
escape.

After she buys and puts on the stockings, she too comes to a
suspension of intellectual thought prior to rebirth of her self:

She was not going through any acute mental process or reasoning with
herself, nor was she striving to explain to her satisfaction the motive of

her action. She was not thinking at all. She seemed for the time to be taking a rest from that laborious and fatiguing function and to have abandoned herself to some mechanical impulse that directed her actions and freed her of responsibility. (502)

She feels, she is sensuously alive, she begins to be her old self made new by her greater enjoyment of self-fulfillment. Of course, tomorrow does come for her just as Brently Mallard did return to Louise. While the realization of her momentary freedom—the pleasure of spending money on herself—and her permanent obligation—her duty to her children—does not kill Mrs. Sommers, she is thrown into a despair from which there is no rescue. For Chopin, there is never an easy resolution to woman's quest for self and fulfillment of desire.

The major stories written immediately prior to Chopin's work on *The Awakening* share this focus on the negativity of unreflective passion as well as Chopin's increasingly complex manipulation of symbols for limitations and despair born out of denied desire. Even as she celebrates the senses as the breaking ground for consciousness, Chopin also portrays the purely sexual as another trap into which both men and women fall, a theme central to Maupassant's "mad" stories that Chopin translated and greatly admired. Desire becomes obsessive passion in these works, and passion proves as much an entrapment, a form of madness, as is ideologically conventional love.

"Her Letters," written 29 November 1894, is important both because it examines male and female responses to passion and because it contains what will become the central image and act of *The Awakening*. In this short story, a woman "pained and savage" with passion goes to destroy her lover's letters (399). It is a leaden day of "no gleam, no rift, no promise" (398), when she can no longer think but only feel and act as a wounded animal would: "With her sharp white teeth she tore the far corner from the letter, where the name was written; she bit the torn scrap and tasted it between her lips and upon her tongue like some god-given morsel" (399). Unable to give up the letters, she entrusts them to her husband's care, willing that he will destroy them without reading a line.

A year later she has died, and on another leaden day of "no

gleam, no promise" (400), her husband finds the letters, suffers a conflict of will about reading them, and finally throws them unopened into a river. His initial discovery illuminates for us the relationship and rift between husband and wife, a point brought home by the bleak refrain, and his later journey to water emphasizes the emptiness of ordinary life and the despair that goes hand in hand with willful nonconsciousness. He realizes that he will never know her true self and that he is forever alienated from her: "The darkness where he stood was impenetrable...leaving him alone in a black, boundless universe" (402). His passion for the now unattainable union and his "man-instinct of possession" (401) lead him to see her as his only salvation: to know "the secret of her existence" (404) will be to know his own self and the meaning of his existence. This desire is the romantic dream of *At Fault* become nightmare, madness, and self-destruction.

It is now that Chopin empowers her water symbol, as will occur in *The Awakening*, here making it the unnatural subject of a madman's obsessive passion to know and to be known by another. The husband returns to the river and the darkness, emasculated by his inability to know, savage in his need for consummation. He believes he hears the call of the water: "It babbled, and he listened to it, and it told him nothing, but it promised all. He could hear it promising him with caressing voice, peace and sweet repose. He could hear the sweep, the song of the water inviting him" (405). He answers by drowning himself, "to join her and her secret thought in the immeasurable rest" (405). Both now "rest" in the same final state but not, as the romantic madman would have it, together; instead, they are forever alienated in death, the ultimate dissolution, just as they were in life. Passion makes no new worlds. The dark side of desire illuminates only the funereal breach of self-faith and the impenetrable state of demented nonconsciousness that passion gives birth to and nurtures. For Chopin, passion alone is eventual self-death and not an avenue toward self-fulfillment.

The themes of mind split from body; dual and conflicting selves; the entrapment of wifehood, motherhood, and sex; the pull of desire and the pain of passion introduced in the stories discussed above will all become central issues in *The Awakening*.

Through the creation of these works, Chopin informed herself of subjects crucial to woman and, at times, men. She taught herself to apprehend and to portray precisely the fissures in the social fabric of her world; she then proceeded to tear apart that neat cover cloth after one last, strange fictional release in a story that both incorporates the last major images of *The Awakening* and remains distanced from the comprehension obtained in that work.

"An Egyptian Cigarette," written in April 1897, is Chopin's concentrated primal version of *The Awakening*, a dream within a tale in which the dreamer escapes the nightmare. Again, Chopin creates a highly unconventional woman and situation that allow a nontragic if perplexing ending. That the female character who dreams is similar to the female writer who creates is obvious; indeed, that the fictional woman maintains a firm grasp of her self-possession despite her visions must have been a desire and dream of her creator as well.

In this short work, a cosmopolitan woman is given a box of Egyptian cigarettes that contain some sort of hallucinogenic drug. She smokes one and immediately experiences a distorted and perverse vision of passion and despair. In the dream, another woman driven wild with longing lies in a desert abandoned by her lover. She, in turn, dreams of following him to entrap him once more with her love. Ensnared by her obsession, she lies dying in the heat and thinks finally only of reaching the river. She also considers the irony of her life and its end: "I laughed at the oracles and scoffed at the stars when they told that after the rapture of life I would open my arms inviting death, and the waters would envelop me" (571). Like Edna at the end of *The Awakening*, she reviews her life, how she lived outside of religion and society for the sake of her love and how she is now abandoned by all. While she is physically tormented by sun and sand, she experiences a momentary shift in consciousness: "It seems to me that I have lain here for days in the sand, feeding upon despair. Despair is bitter and it nourishes resolve" (572). Above her, as will be above Edna, she hears "the wings of a bird flapping above [her] head, flying low, in circles" (572). She too reaches water and goes into it; like Edna she suffers a moment of fear at its embrace, but like Edna, she moves toward resolution and into "the sweet rapture of rest" (572), her senses alive and fulfilled at last.

The dreamer awakens at this point, disoriented and distressed after having thus "tasted the depths of human despair" (572). She contemplates the other dreams waiting for her in the remaining cigarettes: "what might I not find in their mystic fumes? Perhaps a vision of celestial peace; a dream of hopes fulfilled; a taste of rapture, such as had not entered into my mind to conceive" (573). But she is not, finally, a seer. She destroys the cigarettes and is only " 'a little the worse for a dream...' " (573). Chopin, however, did not deny her visions or forget those that had come before. She was moved to final exploration of woman's complicity in her own self-oppression and her ability to overcome self-repression. Two months after writing this story, Chopin began *The Awakening*.

The Awakening, originally entitled "A Solitary Soul" and written between June 1897 and 21 January 1898, begins with an assault on the senses and intellect. A brightly colored parrot caged just outside the door of a Grand Isle resort screams " '*Allez vous-en! Allez vous-en!* Sapristi! That's all right!' " as another pet beside it, a mocking bird, sings "with maddening persistence" (881). Thus, ambiguous warnings and wild elation open Edna Pontellier's experience of self-awakening and Chopin's accounting of the dangers inherent in such attempted self-fulfillment. That Edna's history is tied inextricably to that of men and patriarchal ideology is made clear by the characters introduced first—her husband, children, and future lover. That her story will not be a simply happy one is foreshadowed by the music chosen for the opening, a tune from *Zampa*, a highly sentimental opera of romance and death by water. Furthermore, that Edna is at the point of rebellion, at the moment before the quickening of consciousness, is made evident in the very first pages of this brief but intensely antiromantic work.

Again, Chopin presents us with a woman as outsider, Edna, whose case is made more complex by her apparent security in and attachment to her husband's world. Married to the consummate businessman, Léonce Pontellier, she is accepted in his Creole society as an enchanting if somewhat naive lady. In actuality, she is foreign to that society but simultaneously complicit with the social and sexual business of that world. Hers is, then, an extremely unstable position, based on contingency and her proximity to authority. Raised in Kentucky and Mississippi, she is neither Creole nor part of the old way; instead, she is "an American woman, with a small infusion of French which seemed to have been lost in dilution" (884). Though she is authorized to become part of Creole society by virtue of her marriage, it is markedly clear she is alien: she, unlike the other women in the novel, is named the American way, as *Mrs.* Pontellier. Later, the reader learns that Edna herself is "not thoroughly at home in the society of Creoles" (889), that the supposed freedom of that people coupled with their steady repression of female self-will confuses her. Indeed, she is unlike the other women and, as is pointed out in the first incident of the novel, does not play her ideological roles well.

In the first chapter, Edna has been swimming in the heat of the day with Robert Lebrun, son of the Creole hotel proprietess; a man strikingly similar to Edna in appearance, age, and temperament. This harmless experience coupled with Léonce's annoyance at the womanhood world of leisure leads to a series of accusations and arguments between the Pontelliers. Léonce first admonishes her for her devaluation of the wife self he owns: " 'You are burnt beyond recognition,' he added, looking at his wife as one looks at a valuable piece of personal property which has suffered some damage" (882). She responds by looking at her tanned hands, realizes she lacks her wedding rings, which Léonce is keeping safe for her, and submissively puts them back on, putting on her wifehood role as well. However, Edna cannot long keep up the show of compliance, instead turning her attention to Robert. Léonce then goes to a men's club, returning late in the night and willing to play husband again to Edna. She disappoints him by giving less than full attention to his anecdotes, failing a second time as wife: "He thought it very discouraging that his wife, who was the sole object of his existence, evinced so little interest in things which concerned him, and valued so little his conversation" (885). His second line of attack is to fault her mother self; he tells her a patent lie that one of their sons is deathly ill, and when this elicits no quick response, Léonce "reproached his wife with her inattention, her habitual neglect of the children" (885). In a parodic echo of the birds in the opening—those which, ironically, drove Léonce out of the hotel with their noise—he steadfastly and verbally assaults her in "a monotonous, insistent way" (885) until he drives her from bed and rest. He then sleeps, and, of course, Edna discovers that there is nothing amiss, not, at least, with her children.

This, as Chopin makes clear, is the stuff of normal marriages, incidents such as the above that occur and are as quickly forgiven and forgotten. Léonce, for all his boorishness, is not at all a poor husband. He is a conscientious provider, a distantly affectionate father, a true man who pulls his weight in the business world and expects his familial sphere to give proof of this while offering him respite. According to the standards of hegemonic ideology, he is, in fact, an ideal husband, the truth of which assertion, as Chopin ironically shows, even Edna cannot dispute (887). That he cannot personally understand his wife nor fully "define to his own satisfaction or any one else's wherein his wife failed in her duty toward their children" (887) is perplexing but not, finally, solely his problem. For, as Chopin makes obvious, Léonce's feelings are correct: Edna is not the ideal helpmeet or mother.

Edna is, instead, a solitary soul, "different from the crowd" (894). She is described as young, light, with eyes that are "quick and bright" (883), possessing a clear gaze unencumbered by the spectacles Léonce must wear to correct his vision. She sees things in a markedly different way than others do, albeit not necessarily at first with insight but, on the other hand, with inner sight: "She had a way of turning [her eyes] swiftly upon an object and holding them there as if lost in some inward maze of contemplation or thought" (883). Just so does Edna perceive the first altercation with Léonce; that night she sits alone outside, surrounded by "the everlasting voice of the sea" which comes to her like "a mournful lullaby" (886), and like Chopin's other water creatures, she begins to feel the entrapment of self: "An indescribable oppression, which seemed to generate in some unfamiliar part of her consciousness, filled her whole being with a vague anguish. It was like a shadow, like a mist passing across her soul's summer day. It was strange and unfamiliar; it was a mood" (886). Thus does Edna's apprehension of self begin, as with Chopin's other rebel women, out of a state of physical and spiritual depletion. This self-dramatization, however, is cut short by a too real invasion of mosquitoes. Chopin will not now descend into romanticization unless it be to detail and expose it as such. Her central concern is, instead, to portray the process of willful nonconsciousness giving way to self-consciousness, and despite the sometimes ironic stance of the narrator, she makes clear throughout the difference between reaction and action, stasis and self-discovery. Chopin would have the reader see, just as Edna comes to understand herself, that Edna is feeling but not thinking: "She was just having a good cry all to herself" (888).

Shortly thereafter, Chopin indicates that Edna does begin to think, in part because of her relationships with Adèle Ratignolle and Robert. Adèle is what Edna is not: "a mother-woman" (887), one of the reigning types at Grand Isle. For all Edna's glorification of Adèle—for example, she limns her as a Madonna—Edna also realizes that Adèle is a willing self-martyr: she is one of those "women who idolized their children, worshiped their husbands, and esteemed it a holy privilege to efface themselves as individuals and grow wings as ministering angels" (888). Edna is too much a sensual individualist to deny immediate experience for self-subordination. She is also incapable of devaluing her emotions and playing games of love; her knowledge that Adèle does so—for example, in past flirtations with Robert—merely serves to confuse her. Though drawn to Robert who appears to be almost her male soul, Edna herself cannot play romantically in order to pass the time but must take up with Robert wholeheartedly or not at all; as Adèle later warns Robert, " 'She is not one of us; she is not like us. She might make the unfortunate blunder of taking you seriously' " (900). Since Edna's friends act upon her as living reminders of her self-alienation and limited consciousness, she seeks some individual or entity beyond these to help her understand that which she feels is suffocating her.

The sea which surrounds her, sings to her in her sadness, and engulfs her in "seductive odor" (892) is that which awakens her senses and self. It mirrors her own philosophical predispositions, like the rivers in earlier stories do for their listeners, and offers beyond self-confirmation the sensual promise of self-fulfillment:

The voice of the sea is seductive; never ceasing, whispering, clamoring, murmuring, inviting the soul to wander for a spell in abysses of solitude; to lose itself in mazes of inward contemplation.

The voice of the sea speaks to the soul. The touch of the sea is sensuous, enfolding the body in its soft, close embrace. (893)

Edna continually positions herself near the sea in the Grand Isle sequence so that the sea washes over her senses at all times; as occurs in the sense experiences of the solitary souls in the short stories, it functions both as a projection and reflection of her desire. What it reveals to her is that she cannot lead the dual life of Adèle, cannot be a true woman who willfully sublimates self-desire in self-effacing service to others: "In short, Mrs. Pontellier was beginning to realize her position in the universe as a human being, and to recognize her relations as an individual to the world within and about her" (893). Chopin also indicates that this movement of quickening consciousness cannot be anything but "vague, tangled, chaotic, and exceedingly disturbing" (893) and that, again, process instead of singular revelation is all.

That Edna has from early on been predisposed to pursuing the individual, or exceptional, rather than the socially determined, or sanctioned, life is shown in her childhood remembrances: "Even as a child she had lived her own small life all within herself. At a very early period she had apprehended instinctively the dual life—that outward existence which conforms, the inward life which questions" (893). In other words, she has always been both susceptible to the sensuous and intuitively aware of her circumscribed female existence. Her awakening, however, comes only after intellectual apprehension of what her feelings intimate. First, Edna's attraction to Adèle's beauty and Adèle's sympathetic response to Edna's tentative self-disclosures encourage Edna to explore the continuum of her existence, the past out of which comes her present and on which her future is predicated. Shortly after her confrontation with Léonce, Edna and Adèle sit alone by the sea. Edna stares into the water, and in answer to Adèle's question about her inwardness, she consciously explores the maze of her inner contemplation: " 'I was really not conscious of thinking of anything; but perhaps I can retrace my thoughts' " (896). The sea has made her recall another "sea" of her childhood: she thinks of "a summer day in Kentucky, of a meadow that seemed as big as the ocean to the very little girl walking through the grass which was higher than her waist. She threw out her arms as if swimming when she walked, beating the tall grass as one strikes out in the water" (896). Edna further recalls her childhood awareness of self-limitation: " 'My sun-bonnet obstructed the view. I could see only the stretch of green before me, and I felt as if I must walk on forever, without coming to the end of it' " (896). More importantly, she understands the connection of that self to her present, how her horizons are yet limited and her desire for unobstructed vision bewildering: " 'sometimes I feel this summer as if I were walking through the green meadow again; idly, aimlessly, unthinking and unguided' " (897). Adèle's response is to enclasp Edna's hand, an affectionate but ultimately futile sign of feminine empathy toward the womanhood condition. This first caress, however, serves to provoke Edna's further self-exploration; the sensuous, even in small ways, leads to self-realization and denial of blind, mechanical, or nonreflective behavior.

Edna begins then to analyze for the first time the past, the history of her self-constitution, and she perceives the bases for her self-alienation in her childhood's lacks—her motherlessness and her father's coldness—as well as in her propensity for romantic self-delusion. Her infatuation with unattainable men, most notably and ironically that with a famous tragedian, a man who acts out emotionally, and her business alliance with Léonce only furthered her sense of irrevocable duality: the split between inward and outward expression, her desires set in conflict with social expectations. She had, like so many women, effected the sublimation of her self-will and knowledge by rationalizing the unrealizability of passion, coming to believe that the most life could offer her was passive adoration. Like Désirée, she had settled herself securely in idolness: "As the devoted wife of a man who worshiped her, she felt she would take her place with a certain dignity in the world of reality, closing the portals forever behind her upon the realm of romance and dreams" (898). So too did she take on the role of mother, "a responsibility which

she had blindly assumed and for which Fate had not fitted her"
(899). It is only at the age of twenty-eight, with Adèle by the sea,
that she admits to the dark side of such self-capitulation, that to be
a wife and mother is, for some, only another denial of self-responsibility. She is, however, despite the concern and show of affection
from Adèle and Robert, alone with this realization, and she cannot
as yet take her intuitions a step further toward self-consciousness
until inspirited once more by the sensuous embrace of the sea.

After her experience with Adèle, Edna couples the role of
mother with the call of self, playing with her children by the sea.
One might argue that she becomes a child herself again with
them. So weeks pass, her reality unchanged. Then, at a dinner,
the parrot again shrieks, music from *Zampa* echoes around her,
and Edna experiences another quickening of consciousness.
After dancing, she sits alone on the gallery, halfway between
society and the sea, able to survey both. Mademoiselle Reisz, a
consummate artist in the mold of Paula Von Stoltz, plays Chopin
specifically for her. Since Edna is susceptible to aesthetic sensuousness, music speaks to her in a powerfully subjective way;
she "sees" it and names it. For example, when Adèle played for
her earlier on, Edna entitled the piece "Solitude" and envisioned
a highly romanticized portrait of another solitary soul: "When
she heard it there came before her imagination the figure of a
man standing beside a desolate rock on the seashore. He was
naked. His attitude was one of hopeless resignation as he looked
toward a distant bird winging its flight away from him" (906).
As Anna Shannon Elfenbein argues, Edna's vision is both one
drawn from popular sentimental art and an indication of "her
programming by her culture, a programming she shares with
other women encouraged to visualize themselves as men in order
to attain vicarious individuality and to adopt a negative view of
the potential of women as well" (146). However, when Reisz
plays, Edna does not see a discrete, displaced rendering of her
sexual alienation or romantic fatalism; instead, because she is
predisposed "to take an impress of the abiding truth" (906), she
feels self-will and desire: "She saw no pictures of solitude, of
hope, of longing, or of despair. But the very passions themselves
were aroused within her soul, swaying it, lashing it, as the waves
daily beat upon her splendid body" (906). This time Edna en-

clasps another woman's hand, and thus is created another female
world, unlike Adèle's, which will inform and urge Edna forward
in her quest for self. This show of deep sympathy and self-
exposure readies Edna for the monstrous joy she embraces in
her moonlight swim that night.

Up to this point, Edna, not surprisingly, cannot swim nor can
anyone succeed in teaching her. It is the individual nature of
the act and not its physicality which frightens her: "A certain
ungovernable dread hung about her when in the water, unless
there was a hand near by that might reach out and reassure her"
(908). Those fears now leave her, and, indeed, she desires precisely the singularity that intimidated her before: "A feeling of
exultation overtook her, as if some power of significant import
had been given her to control the working of her body and her
soul. She grew daring and reckless, overestimating her strength.
She wanted to swim far out, where no woman had swum before"
(908). She does swim out alone, searching for "space and solitude" (908) by gazing at the moonlit horizon, and, finally, she
reaches "for the unlimited in which to lose herself" (908). That
she does not seek physical annihilation is made clear by her
momentary terror of death by drowning. Edna desires to embrace self and, simultaneously, to free herself from womanhood
bonds. To that effect, she leaves the swimmers and walks home
alone, claiming her experience as her own despite the private
self-congratulation of the others. She also rejects Robert's myth-
making, his romantic reading of her swim, determined instead
to value and to reach an understanding of the "thousand emotions [that] have swept through [her]" (909). She does, however,
allow Robert, her sometime psychic twin, to sit with her in the
night and to become part of her self-desire.

That night, the second confrontation between Edna and
Léonce occurs, but this time Edna is not oppressed by his pos-
sessiveness and stubbornness. She refuses to go to their bed,
preferring to rest outside so that she can hear the sound of the
sea. She is not asleep as in the first altercation; she is in fact
intensely awake and alert to her dual life staring her in the face
as Léonce commands her in:

She perceived that her will had blazed up, stubborn and resistant. She
could not at that moment have done other than denied and resisted.

She wondered if her husband had ever spoken to her like that before, and if she had submitted to his command. Of course she had; she remembered that she had. But she could not realize why or how she should have yielded, feeling as she then did. (912)

This time she does not weep, and there are no mosquitoes. Instead, she experiences physical and mental fatigue coupled with the insistent and irritating presence of Léonce hovering about her:

Edna began to feel like one who awakens gradually out of a dream, a delicious, grotesque, impossible dream, to feel again the realities pressing into her soul. The physical need for sleep began to overtake her; the exuberance which had sustained and exalted her spirit left her helpless and yielding to the conditions which crowded her in. (912)

After this and in the face of seemingly insurmountable obstacles, Edna will attempt to make her fleeting vision of self-fulfillment a reality.

She begins by recapitulating her past, this time willfully forcing every experience to its ultimate conclusion. Edna has first been a babe in the sea, moving from childlike helplessness and submissiveness to a preconsciousness of her sensuality and self. She next relives her romantic adolescence, this time with a supposedly attainable man, Robert.

The day following her swim, Edna moves into another state of unreflective reaction and frenzied action: "She was blindly following whatever impulse moved her, as if she had placed herself in alien hands for direction, and freed her soul of responsibility" (913). She calls Robert to her for the first time, and together they leave for an out island, a lovers' haven. Edna now seems to accept Robert's romantic vision of herself and revels in their shared experience in near solitude: they are together outside the Creole society both seem to reject, in another world in which their coupled experience is nurtured. Edna, fatigued after her awakening in the sea the night before, reenacts a female version of the Sleeping Beauty tale: she goes to a pure white room within sound of "the voice of the sea" (917), lies in a virginally white bed, and perceives her own body "as if it were something she saw for the first time, the fine, firm quality and

texture of her flesh" (918). She awakens herself. Robert tells her
later that she has slept "precisely one hundred years" (919).
Chopin indicates here, however, that Edna's romantic chatter is
self-ironic and idle play; Robert is and remains the one true
romantic. In fact, Edna is more radical than sentimental. While
Robert would be her constant and unchanging prince-lover,
Edna envisions massive social transformation which would leave
them both behind: " 'How many years have I slept?' she inquired.
'The whole island seems changed. A new race of beings must
have sprung up, leaving only you and me as past relics' " (919).

Despite their different readings of their shared experience,
Edna finds that this journey, this adventure, revitalizes her desire
for a new self. After their return, she sees again that her singular
though still limited insight has changed her forever:

> she tried to discover wherein this summer had been different from any
> and every other summer of her life. She could only realize that she
> herself—her present self—was in some way different from the other
> self. That she was seeing with different eyes and making the acquain-
> tance of new conditions in herself that colored and changed her en-
> vironment, she did not yet suspect. (921)

Edna need not then realize in full her life's permanent alteration
since her social relations, even her romantic attachment, at
Grand Isle still reflect that society's expectations. It is only when
the unusual occurs, when Robert abruptly departs for Mexico,
that Edna faces how unconsciously she had expected him to
remain a part of her immediate world, her key to her inner self.
Edna must now define her feelings, although in doing so she
senses self-inadequacy, as well as determine how inextricably
bound her new self is to her relationship with Robert:

> For the first time she recognized anew the symptoms of infatuation
> which she had felt incipiently as a child, as a girl in her earliest teens,
> and later as a young woman. The recognition did not lessen the reality,
> the poignancy of the revelation by any suggestion or promise of inst-
> ability. The past was nothing to her; offered no lesson which she was
> willing to heed. The future was a mystery which she never attempted
> to penetrate. The present alone was significant; was hers, to torture
> her as it was doing then with the biting conviction that she had lost that

which she had held, that she had been denied that which her impassioned, newly awakened being demanded. (927)

She is in the adolescence of her new life.

After Robert's abandonment, Edna returns to the primal scene, the originary setting of her new self, the sea which offers her now "the only real pleasurable moments that she knew" (927). She also grows increasingly obsessed with any traces of Robert—photos, letters, anecdotes—since this fetishism both keeps at bay her dull existence as Mrs. Pontellier and continuously reminds her by association of her rediscovered self-will and desire. In addition, she protects her inner self from violation and is virtually untouchable, especially with her husband and children. Only at the end of her vacation is she forced into a relationship with someone, Reisz, a relationship which becomes crucial later on since Reisz sees both Robert and Edna in a radically different way. In the meantime, however, Edna moves to another reenactment of her dual existence.

Edna next takes up again her roles as wife and mother as the Pontelliers return to New Orleans. The latter part is particularly shortlived since even at Grand Isle Edna made clear that she would not subsume self in motherhood:

Edna had once told Madame Ratignolle that she would never sacrifice herself for her children, or for any one.... "I would give up the unessential; I would give my money, I would give my life for my children; but I wouldn't give myself. I can't make it more clear; it's only something which I am beginning to comprehend, which is revealing itself to me." (929)

Neither can she long sustain the illusion of herself as devoted wife. She rejects the simple social conventions of reception days, thus withdrawing her interest from her husband's business. The materialistic base of the Pontellier marriage is then exposed when Léonce attacks her both for hurting his business by neglecting hers and for mismanaging his familial establishment. As Brian Lee argues:

The conspicuous consumption satirized by Veblen is the visible corollary of Edna's feelings of uselessness and futility. In order to maintain her husband's financial credibility, her role in their marriage is reduced to that of chief ornament in his display of wealth. The rules of their stylized existence permit her to take but not to make. Her creative instincts are stifled, and the need which Perkins [Gilman] argues is the distinguishing characteristic of humanity—to express one's inner thoughts in some outer form—is denied her. (66)

Despite the insensitivity of Léonce's responses to her actions, throughout their confrontations, Edna now deliberately tries to maintain her self-composure. However, after one such argument, she retires to her room and there attempts a reversal of her initial submissiveness: she tries to crush underfoot her wedding ring. Her failure to do so—the maid hands it back to her undamaged, and she puts it on—implicitly discloses that the individual cannot so easily erase the past, one's complicity with self-objectification. Although Edna does not yet conceive of an alternative to her society, she clearly sees the vacuity of the old ways.

Indeed, like Louise Mallard, Edna at first romanticizes her relationship to the real world beyond her window but instead of seeing it as a green world inviting her to it, she perceives it as the enemy in her quest for self-constitution: "She felt no interest in anything about her. The street, the children, the fruit vendor, the flowers growing there under her eyes, were all part and parcel of an alien world which had suddenly become antagonistic" (935). Even when she considers the seeming faultlessness of Adèle's marriage and domestic sphere, she cannot accept that ideological role and realm as holding for her the possibility of self-fulfillment. It is after her visit to Adèle that she gives up all pretense of social conformity and is then judged insane by Léonce, though not by the narrator or resisting reader: "He could see plainly that she was not herself. That is, he could not see that she was becoming herself and daily casting aside that fictitious self which we assume like a garment with which to appear before the world" (939).

Edna's process of self-realization begins in earnest with yet another recapitulation of experience. She turns to her art for which she has a "natural aptitude" (891) but which before was mere "dabbling" (891). She now takes it up seriously in an at-

tempt to articulate herself; as she tells Adèle, " 'I believe I ought
to work again. I feel as if I wanted to be doing something' "
(937). Again, this action provokes Léonce into an attack on her.
For him, her work should fall within prescribed womanhood
roles; the artistic impulse can be icing on the cake but should
never be the full repast. Edna, alienated from family and friends,
then turns to Mademoiselle Reisz, and it is in this confrontation
that Edna is offered the life possibilities available to her.

Edna tracks down Reisz through Madame Lebrun who also
passes on inconsequential news of Robert. In sharp contrast to
Lebrun, Reisz has only significant words for Edna. Theirs is not
like the polite, reserved conversation between Edna and the Le-
bruns. They face each other without pretense of affection and
are ultimately revealed to each other as kindred souls housed in
arrestingly dissimilar bodies. Reisz in essence seduces Edna into
self-recognition; she strokes her hand, nurtures her body, heart,
and soul by feeding her, giving her a highly revealing letter from
Robert, and playing again Chopin's "Impromptu," recalling for
Edna the "one midnight at Grand Isle when strange, new voices
awoke in her" (946). More importantly, Reisz speaks seriously
with and to Edna of her " 'becoming an artist' ":

[Reisz says,] "To be an artist includes much; one must possess many
gifts—absolute gifts—which have not been acquired by one's own effort.
And, moreover, to succeed, the artist must possess the courageous soul."

"What do you mean by the courageous soul?"

"Courageous, *ma foi!* The brave soul. The soul that dares and defies."
(946)

Because Reisz feels deeply for Edna, loves her for reasons left
unexplored in the text, she feeds both Edna's desire and self-
desire even as she herself feeds upon Edna's passion. Edna discovers through her the two paths from which she must choose:
one is to surrender herself to romance with Robert and by that
act to move away from self-fulfillment; the other is to rebel
completely, following Reisz's example, to give up body and soul
to the new life. The remainder of the novel focuses on these two
alternatives and Edna's growing consciousness of how limited
these life options are. Herein lies Chopin's most acute social

criticism, that which shocked her contemporaries and still proves stunning today.

In essence, Chopin has Edna come to realize that there are no life options for her which afford her more than the illusion of satisfaction or the reality of self-compromise. To be a mother-woman is to abjure self for the sake of others; to be an artist-woman is to live celibate, to give all one's love to expression. Edna proves incapable of sustaining herself in such solitude, no matter how peaceful it seems for a while. Instead, she would be part of the world: "It was not despair, but it seemed to her as if life were passing by, leaving its promise broken and unfulfilled. Yet there were other days when she listened, was led on and deceived by fresh promises which her youth held out to her" (956). Edna's weakness, then, is her desire for action coupled with her own conditioned passivity, her desire for experience coupled with her ignorance of life. She hungers for "something to happen—something, anything; she did not know what" (958) but cannot herself initiate action to effect that occurrence. Instead, she is drawn repeatedly to the dynamic world of men seemingly unlike those she has known. Thus she becomes even more entrapped in a mire of self-deception.

Since both Robert and Léonce leave her, Edna is "free" to explore "the animalism" (961) awakened in her. She takes up with Alcée Arobin, a well-known libertine, and is drawn to him both because of his forceful sensualness and his extremely passionate nature. Early on she discovers his duelling scar, an insignificant mark itself save that it perhaps reflects her own love wounds and her duelling selves: "He stood close to her, and the effrontery in his eyes repelled the old, vanishing self in her, yet drew all her awakening sensuousness" (959). Even though Edna understands that he is "absolutely nothing to her" (960), he too acts as both reminder of and respite from her struggle with self-consciousness. Her naivety is such that she initially believes his presence will offer some sort of self-illumination; her affair does insofar as it makes her aware of her renunciation of "all the codes" through which she has identified herself (966). However, she also discovers, too late, that his is a world of deception and not compassion. She learns as well that her natural sensuality is not "devilishly wicked" (966) but that she has wasted her expression of self in the alienating experience of passion:

> She felt as if a mist had been lifted from her eyes, enabling her to look upon and comprehend the significance of life, that monster made up of beauty and brutality. But among the conflicting sensations which assailed her, there was neither shame nor remorse. There was a dull pang of regret because it was not the kiss of love which had inflamed her, because it was not love which had held this cup of life to her lips. (967)

After their first night together, then, Edna comprehends that this path, passion become entrapment, is another dead end. As Rosemary F. Franklin points out, "Chopin shrewdly designs the Alcée episode to present what will be Edna's greatest challenge: to understand that romantic love is born of the erotic longing within oneself for transcendence that cannot be fulfilled by union with another human being" (523). Though their relationship continues, Edna feels nothing, neither "despondency" nor "hope" (988). It is not the way for her to self.

Edna's other alternative, one which she actively pursues for some time, is to immerse herself in art, in her case notably a world made up of women, hoping to find the means to self-expression. This world is neatly divorced at times from that of men—she will not allow Arobin into her atelier—and it is based on ruthless honesty. Turning away from her lover, Edna finds the deepest satisfaction in her relationship with that other one who recalls her to true self: Reisz, "the woman, by her divine art, seemed to reach Edna's spirit and set it free" (961). While Edna philosophizes with Arobin about her self-discovery, she discusses pragmatics with Reisz. Edna speaks first to her of her resolution "never again to belong to another than herself" (963) and her decision to have rooms of her own, supporting herself with her mother's legacy and money earned from sale of her own art. She also openly admits to her love for Robert and is warned by Reisz that he is but another ordinary man, like Léonce, who wants to have her " 'belong to him' " (964). Reisz speaks to Edna as well of her need for union with another, that which she has herself not been able to effect; she tells Edna to search for a man of " 'some *grand esprit*; a man with lofty aims and ability to reach them; one who stood high enough to attract the notice of his fellow-men' " (964). Finally, Reisz forces Edna to contemplate anew a life of solitude—and, one surmises, celibacy—as an alternative. The true artist who gives voice to self is one who can stand alone; as Reisz tells Edna, " 'The bird that would soar above the level plain of tradition and prejudice must have strong wings. It is a sad spectacle to see the weaklings bruised, exhausted, fluttering back to earth' " (966). Even though Chopin surrounds Edna with such deep sympathy, and though it is clear that Edna now desires self-expression and transcendence of the oppressive ordinary, the reader is also made aware that Edna is "devoid of ambition" (956), yet too passive to effect revolution.

Edna herself becomes fully conscious of this fact at her last dinner at the Pontellier home. She is feted by friends and lovers, is about to move to her own residence, is proving successful as an artist, seems, in short, to be beginning a new life on this her twenty-ninth birthday. However, she is also crowned by Léonce's jewels and toasted with a concoction made by her father especially for "the daughter whom he invented" (971). Furthermore, Arobin's dramatic self-presence suggests that she is yet still possessed. Even her closest friend, her confidante Reisz, is revealed as inadequate to the situation; as Susan Resneck Parr argues, Reisz's size and childlike seating at the table upon a pile of cushions indicate that Reisz also "has failed to achieve her maturity" (145). Edna sees her bacchanal for the "stupid" (976) debacle it is. Her "*coup d'état*" fails (969).

Despite a brief reunion with her children and Adèle, Edna moves herself after this into the solitary life, even though she knows herself incapable of maintaining such independence or self-possession. There is seemingly only one other path left open to her at this point: her reunion with Robert, whom she believes to be Reisz's man of grand esprit. They meet by accident at Reisz's apartment, and there begins Edna's final self-deception. Her idealistic visions of him and their relationship are first undercut by the awkward reality of chance encounter, trivial chatter, Robert's reticence and evasiveness. Once he accompanies her home, she finds him to be momentarily "like the old Robert" (983) but later admits to herself that in "some way he had seemed nearer to her off there in Mexico" (987). He, in turn, finds her "cruel" (984), a mimic of his romantic self. Their relationship is further complicated by mutual jealousy, his over Arobin and hers over his Vera Cruz woman. Robert also avoids her until she confronts him with his "selfishness" (990) and seduces him into giving her that which he has been saving for himself. Edna expects this "something" (990) to be a desire equal to her own; instead, as Reisz foresaw, Robert reveals his man-instinct of possession. He wishes to be her husband, and it is impossible for the reader not to recall that for Robert those who are married are never lovers (915). When Robert tells Edna he desires that she be given to him as wife, she then reveals herself as beyond his understanding: she says, " 'You have been a very, very foolish boy, wasting your time dreaming of impossible things when you speak of Mr. Pontellier setting me free! I am no longer one of Mr. Pontellier's possessions to dispose of or not. I give myself where I choose' " (992). However, Edna's ability to articulate or to live out her superior sense of self is contingent upon Robert's reflecting that self to her. So that she might perhaps capture whole the truth of her singularity, she invests herself once more in achieving a relationship with him. In doing so, Edna misjudges or chooses not to recognize Robert's motives or his ability to "hold against her own passion" (987). That Robert does not prove equal to her desire is made obvious in his abandonment of her. One might also argue, as Rosemary F. Franklin does, that because Edna "has projected her awakening animus upon him and thus is unable to know him as an individual," he flees from her (515). His parting note to her, however, suggests another interpretation: that because she will not act as his mirror, will not reflect the primacy of his desire, he goes: " 'I love you. Good-by—because I love you' " (997). Ironically, his desertion is "necessary" (999). It marks the end of the battle between Edna's "need for consciousness" and Robert's desire to maintain "the comfortable status quo" of unconsciousness (Franklin 514).

Edna comes then to realize that the world of womanhood is for her also a potentially deadly one. She sits by Adèle during her delivery and is deeply affected by what this reveals to her.

During the birth of her own children, she had been put to sleep; she thus experiences the reality of childbearing for the first time, albeit from the distanced vantage point of spectator. This scene of suffering makes her apprehend at last what passion might effect: "Edna did not go. With an inward agony, with a flaming, outspoken revolt against the ways of Nature, she witnessed the scene of torture" (995). In this world, her body is her destiny, another means of entrapment. Chopin's description of Adèle's long hair lying "coiled like a golden serpent" (994) reminds the reader of woman's seduction in and expulsion from Paradise, the curse of childbirth given to her as her burden. The novel's structure also promotes such a reading: Edna's own nine-month gestation of self coupled with Adèle's pregnancy inextricably links woman's self-desire with self-accommodation.

After Adèle has given birth and even though Edna is deadened by fatigue, Edna comprehends that she can no longer amateurishly dabble at any of the womanhood roles available to her— martyr, beautiful object, social capital, the beloved; she also feels that such self-alienation is not too high a price to pay for self-knowledge if one thus be freed of the illusions that merely serve as "a decoy to secure mothers for the race": " 'Yes,' she said. 'The years that are gone seem like dreams—if one might go on sleeping and dreaming—but to wake up and find—oh! well! perhaps it is better to wake up after all, even to suffer, rather than to remain a dupe to illusions all one's life' " (996). Robert's letter and second abandonment occasion her final moment of disillusionment, the experience of which sends her, depleted spiritually and physically, back to Grand Isle, almost nine months after her first awakening in the sea. Here in the Gulf, "the repository and graveyard of legend and dreams" (Taylor 177), she will at last deliver herself.

Edna thinks before she returns there, analyzing her search for subjectivity and her subjection, her sensuality and the dangers of sexuality. When she reaches Grand Isle, she is beyond contemplation and no longer duelling with incompatible selves. She has given up trying to communicate with those she loves or who love her. In this last chapter, she answers instead the voice of the sea which now calls her into eternal "abysses of solitude"

(999), not of contemplation but of momentary self-possession followed by self-annihilation. Chopin's imagery expresses both Edna's alienation and singularity. She stands alone and defeated in her struggle to affirm her selfhood to others: "A bird with a broken wing was beating the air above, reeling, fluttering, circling disabled down, down to the water" (999). Yet Edna transcends despair, if only by embracing death.

Edna had said earlier that she "would give up the unessential" (929) but not herself. Now she throws aside her life as easily as she does her old bathing suit so that she might feel "like some new-born creature, opening its eyes in a familiar world that it had never known" (1000). Like Venus returning to her originary scene, she descends into the sea, re-experiencing for the last time her childhood motherlessness, adolescent infatuation, the terrors and exhaustion of womanhood. She reaches then for a state of pure liminality, a prelapsarian world, one in which she might experience sensual transcendence, herself become one with nature, "the hum of bees, and the musky odor of pinks" (1000). Edna has only one experience that is not compromised, the fleeting moment of intense life force she embraces before drowning; that this experience necessarily leads to her death is Chopin's most radical statement about and to her civilized, genteel world.

Edna's defeat, her surrender of self to the abysses of solitude, is a profoundly despairing and desperate measure. Hers is not the beautiful death of romantic heroines, nor does Chopin write it as such; instead, Chopin focuses attention to the last line on Edna's desire for life, her fragmented, inexpressible desire for autonomy, and her inability to find subject position within a world in which a woman's life is deemed unessential even by herself. Yet one also sees in Edna's life, as one does in much of Chopin's fiction, intimations of alternatives to alienation and self-annihilation, a new "structure of feeling," as Raymond Williams called it, an embryonic social consciousness which cannot yet be fully articulated either by character or creator (131–132). Edna's death is unspeakable tragedy, yet one does hear in her story the constant murmur, whisper, clamor of another vision of life. Through her work, Chopin invites the reader to imagine a world in which woman's experience and desire are no longer marginalized or effaced but have become critically central. In this way, as Judi Roller writes, *The Awakening* is "a fitting prelude to the twentieth-century's feminist novels" (28).

5

Edith Wharton's Life and Art

Edith Wharton was born in 1862 and died in 1937, or, as Vito
J. Brenni writes, she was "born during the American Civil War
and died in the same year in which, the late George Orwell was
convinced, 'history ended' " (x). Her family was related to the
Rhinelander and Schermerhorn-Jones clans whose money came
chiefly from real estate speculation. Though her upbringing was
genteel, her family's social standing was on the lowest rung of
the New York 400. Wharton received no formal schooling but
was privately educated by her father and governesses; indeed,
her mother considered literature so inherently spurious that
Wharton was not to read contemporary fiction until after her
marriage. Due to economic depressions after the Civil War,
Wharton's family chose to live abroad, where American money
went further, and the greater part of her childhood was spent
touring the Continent. She married Edward Robbins Wharton
of the Boston aristocracy in 1885 and was divorced from him in
1913 after his long and traumatic decline into insanity. After
1913, she returned to the United States for only one brief visit,
preferring instead residency in France.

During World War I, Wharton was actively involved in charity
work and used her social connections to help finance workshops
for unemployed seamstresses, the American Hostels for Refu-
gees, The Children of Flanders Rescue Committee, and several
American Convalescent Homes. At the same time, she worked

as a war correspondent, an exceptionally rare position for a
woman, for the New York presses. For her war work, she was
made a Chevalier of the French Legion of Honor and awarded
both the Medal of Queen Elizabeth and the Order of Leopold
by Belgium. Similarly, she amassed rare honors for her work in
fiction. In 1921, she was awarded the Pulitzer Prize, the first
given to a woman, for *The Age of Innocence*. It was, however, an
honor tinged with compromise as the Pulitzer was given to Wharton, the choice of the Columbia University trustees, only in order
that it not be given to Sinclair Lewis, the original choice of the
jury. In 1924, Wharton again broke tradition when she was
granted an honorary degree of Doctor of Letters by Yale University. Also in that year, she became the second novelist, following W. D. Howells, and the second woman, after Julia Ward
Howe, to be recognized by the presentation of a Gold Medal
from the American Academy of Arts and Letters.

Her writing career, like that of Chopin, is notable at first in-
spection for its early beginnings, long hiatus, and late fruition.
This pattern was due in great part to her social background and
upbringing; as Wharton wrote in her memoirs, *A Backward
Glance*: "In the eyes of our provincial society authorship was still
regarded as something between a black art and a form of manual
labour" (68–69). This upper-class prejudice against the craft of
literature remained constant throughout her life and was made
evident to her through various forms of social censure. Wharton
wrote, for example, of being invited early on in her career to a
party at which a "Bohemian artist" would be introduced; she
was more than a little astonished to find herself pointed out as
that same artist. Wharton also wrote of the social ostracism incurred as a consequence of her writing "scandalous" novels: "I
remember once saying that I was a failure in Boston (where we
used to go to stay with my husband's family) because they
thought I was too fashionable to be intelligent; and a failure in
New York because they were afraid I was too intelligent to be
fashionable" (*Backward Glance* 119). Indeed, Wharton's career
was almost nipped in the bud at its earliest stage when in 1873,
at the age of twelve, she presented her first novel to her mother
who read the opening sentences and told her that the portrayal
of manners therein was incorrect and unseemly. The novel was

destroyed. Despite such an inauspicious beginning and the later continual criticism from all sides, Wharton became a professional writer and maintained an active career into her seventies, leaving unfinished at her death her potentially greatest work, *The Buccaneers*.

Wharton wrote her second novel at the age of fourteen for a girlfriend. *Fast and Loose*, found among her private papers, is notable chiefly for the bogus reviews Wharton wrote and appended to it. Her satiric wit and her attitude toward critics were already sharp as can readily be seen in lines taken from the mock *Nation* review: "The English of it is that every character is a failure, the plot a vacuum, the style spiritless, the dialogue vague, the sentiments weak, & the whole thing a fiasco" (121). *Fast and Loose* was a purely personal undertaking (which later became an elaborate private joke, appearing in various reincarnations in several short stories). Wharton did not attempt serious fiction again until 1890. Instead, she turned to poetry, some of which was published at her own expense and some promoted by established presses when she was seventeen. Her poetry was conventional at its best; one reads the poems as documents of apprenticeship and not as early unappreciated masterpieces.

After her marriage, Wharton began work on a series of short stories, many of which were published separately between 1891–1899. During that period, she also co-authored, with Ogden Codman, Jr., a book on interior design entitled *The Decoration of Houses* that was and still is considered radical in its aesthetic pronouncements. Ever interested in form and style, as can be seen in her later studies of Italy and France, Wharton found this type of work amusing but noted that it "can hardly be regarded as a part of my literary career" (*Backward Glance* 112). Her three short story collections—*The Greater Inclination* (1899), *Crucial Instances* (1901), and *The Descent of Man, and Other Stories* (1904)—and her first two novellas—*The Touchstone* (1900) and *Sanctuary* (1903)—were more serious literary endeavors. Still, for Wharton, they were beginner's material treated in a novice's manner. Nor did she consider her first major work, *The Valley of Decision* (1902), a personal artistic success:

"The Valley of Decision" was not, in my sense of the term, a novel at all, but only a romantic chronicle, unrolling its episodes like the frescoed legends on the palace-walls which formed its background; my idea of a novel was something very different, something far more compact and centripetal, and I doubted whether I should ever have enough constructive power to achieve anything beyond isolated character studies, or the stringing together of picturesque episodes. (*Backward Glance* 205)

Wharton, then, was aware of the necessary development of technical skills as well as that of her own formulated aesthetic code. While many of her early stories were brilliant examples of "disengaging of crucial instances from the welter of existence" (*Writing of Fiction* 14), she was still searching for focused style and subject, a cogent moral philosophy to express through her particular brand of the novel of manners. She succeeded, in major ways, in resolving technical and aesthetic problems in her first bestseller, *The House of Mirth* (1905).

In a 1918 letter to Victor Solberg, Wharton pointed out that "every dawning talent has to go through a phase of initiation & subjection to influences, & the great object of the young writer should be, not to fear these influences, but to seek only the greatest, & to assimilate them so that they become part of his stock-in-trade" (*Letters* 411). As is documented in her *The Writing of Fiction* (1925), Wharton believed her own major influences to be European, as well as the works of some radical American authors. She particularly admired and emulated the social fiction of Balzac, Stendhal, Tolstoy, and George Eliot which agreed with her precept that "the bounds of a personality are not reproducible by a sharp black line, but that each of us flows imperceptibly into adjacent people and things" (7), a construct not far from Chopin's own belief in psychological symbolism. Further, for Wharton, such works, as well as those by Whitman, exemplified her major theory of selection and organization. For her, form and content were indistinguishably one:

There seems to be but two primary questions to ask in estimating any work of art: what has the author tried to represent, and how far has he succeeded?—and a third, which is dependent on them: Was the subject chosen worth representing—has it the quality of being what Balzac called "vrai dans l'art"? These three inquiries, if duly pressed, yield a full answer to the aesthetic problem of the novel. Outside of them no criticism can be either relevant or interesting, since it is only by viewing the novel as an organic whole, by considering its form and function as one, that the critic can properly estimate its details of style and construction. ("Criticism of Fiction" 230)

In brief, Wharton believed that once an author's moral or social statement was established in the mind, the proper form for its effective presentation would become evident. Wharton, then, unlike James, had no set rules of design. In fact, she found James's theories of concentrated point of view and symmetric construction prescriptive and stultifying; similarly, she criticized the concept of dominating plot as banal. Nor did she find the proletarian or Naturalist movements always progressive: for her, these tended to produce works which were mechanical, nonselective, critically inept and morally suspect. Instead, Wharton favored a mild form of aesthetic anarchism: "General rules of art are useful chiefly as a lamp in a mine, or a hand-rail down a black stairway; they are necessary for the sake of the guidance they give, but it is a mistake, once they are formulated, to be too much in awe of them" (*Writing of Fiction* 42). More explicitly, and more typical of Wharton the shrewd businesswoman, she wrote, "There is no fixed rule about this, or about any other method; each in the art of fiction, to justify itself has only to succeed" (100).

By 1905, Wharton was aware of the need for a further sharpening of her subject matter and social philosophy; as she wrote later, "In the House of Art are many mansions, and the novelist's business is to stick to the one in which he feels himself at home" ("Cycle of Reviewing" 45). Wharton's home, both figuratively and literally, was New York society, whether it be in New York or abroad, in the 400 itself or wherever its conventions touched and were observed. She felt strongly the need to "write about what I see, what I happen to be nearest to" (*Letters* 91). Some of her early stories centered on various incidents within this society; but it was obvious to Wharton that these situations lacked necessary significance for expansion into novel-length treatments. Wharton wrote, in *A Backward Glance*, of her search for a truly "crucial instance":

In what aspect could a society of irresponsible pleasure-seekers be said to have, on the "old woe of the world," any deeper bearing than the people composing such a society could guess? The answer was that a frivolous society can acquire dramatic significance only through what its frivolity destroys. Its tragic implication lies in its power of debasing people and ideals. The answer, in short, was my heroine, Lily Bart. (207)

Wharton had found her centripetal subject and philosophical stance: "Such groups always rest on an underpinning of wasted human possibilities; and it seemed to me that the fate of the persons embodying these possibilities ought to redeem my subject from insignificance" (*House of Mirth* vii). Thus Wharton set her hierarchy of values with *The House of Mirth*. That hierarchy would be much misunderstood by her early critics.

That Wharton's work stands as a link between nineteenth- and twentieth-century literary and cultural sensibilities is a common observation. It is customary to place her in the traditional and progressive Howells-James-Fitzgerald line; or, as Michael Millgate has astutely observed:

Edith Wharton occupies an extremely important intermediary position between James and Fitzgerald: indeed, we might argue that Fitzgerald could hardly have written *The Great Gatsby* without *The Custom of the Country*, and it is beyond argument that *The Custom of the Country* itself could not have been written without the whole body of James's achievement behind it. (63)

Beyond this elementary point, however, there is little critical agreement. Indeed, to paraphrase an early critic's jab at Wharton, in many cases it seemed to be the critics' only aim to dish Wharton "for the sake of the sensation of dishing her" (Hackett 39). Wharton's work, from its publication date to the present day, has been criticized for its supposed dated content and reactionary philosophy. Marilyn Jones Lyde, in her 1959 study of Wharton, sums up the situation well:

Too liberal for the Victorians, she was overly moralistic for twentieth-century naturalism. Worst of all, from the modern point of view, she was writing of the wrong class; in a period which the critics like to describe as an age of brute struggle for survival, she continued to concern herself with the nice moral issues which confront the privileged set and have nothing to do with the rise of the masses or the union demand for a higher wage. (xv)

More recently, in his 1978 introduction to *The Edith Wharton Omnibus*, Gore Vidal has spoken against a more personal bias evident in criticism on her: "Due to her sex, class (in every sense), and place of residence, she has been denied her proper place in the near-empty pantheon of American literature" (vii). A brief overview of major critical responses will make clear the need for a total reevaluation of Wharton's stature as writer and social critic.

Ironically enough, it is Henry James who must bear partial blame for the critical biases against Wharton. James became a close friend of hers in 1903 and remained so until his death. However, their critical disagreements were many; their friendship was certainly not that between master and disciple. By the mid–1900s, Wharton was already staggering under the weighty title of "Great American Author" or considered, at least, as the greatest woman writer of her day. James read her first two books in 1902 and, in a much-quoted letter, wrote that he wanted only "to get hold of the little lady and pump the pure essence of my wisdom and experience into her. She *must* be tethered in native pastures, even if it reduces her to a back-yard in New York" (James's *Letters* 396). He also spoke of her "cleverness," a label that coupled with the equally if subtly condescending term "brilliancy" would haunt her throughout her career. Later, in James's important review of *The Custom of the Country*, he further set her up for critical misreading by praising Wharton's "particular fine asperity" as her chief literary virtue, extrapolating that talent into, what seems now, a sort of literary transvestism:

A shade of asperity may be in such fashion a security against waste, and in the dearth of displayed securities we should welcome it on that ground alone. It helps at any rate to constitute for the talent manifest in "The Custom" a rare identity, so far should we have to go to seek another instance of the dry, or call it perhaps even the hard, intellectual touch in the soft, or call it perhaps even the humid, temperamental air; in other words of the masculine conclusion tending so to crown the feminine observation. ("The New Novel" 356)

Single-handedly, then, James promulgated the myths of her dis-
cipleship to him, the qualification that her genius relied upon
regionalist limitation, and the superiority of masculine sensibility
to feminine sensitivity. Unfortunately, these biases remained
powerful, in varying degrees of intensity, until very recently.

James, of course, was writing in tune with the times, supporting the nineteenth-century concepts of womanhood and art,
as well as in defense of his own aesthetic formulations and, at
that time, as a reaction to his waning popularity. His true dis-
ciples, who were many, carried on his, as it were, critical damning
with faint praise. As Katherine Joslin points out, one of Wharton's great mistakes was to select Gaillard Lapsley as her literary
executor since he then chose Percy Lubbock as her biographer.
Lubbock, "her one-time friend but long-term foe," believed her
to be inferior to James and unlikely to be given attention by
more than her generation and of that group only the women
(193–194). Lubbock then wrote *Portrait of Edith Wharton* (1947),
which was labelled a critical biography but reads, rather, as a
snappish personal attack on Wharton as a woman and Wharton
as an impatient and limited student of the Master. A majority
of 1950s criticism continued in the same vein; at that time, interest in literary technique was paramount, and both James and
Fitzgerald reigned supreme in the pantheon of form. Wharton
was interesting only as a somewhat dulled mirror image of
James's technical precepts, and her work was not viewed as original either in form or in content. This traditional attitude began
to break down only with the publication of Millicent Bell's *Edith
Wharton & Henry James: The Story of Their Friendship* (1965), in
which Bell disproved Lubbock's assertion that Wharton "was
herself a novel of [James's], no doubt in his earliest manner"
(21). However, many 1960s critics, such as the self-labelled Jacobite Louis Auchincloss, upheld to some degree the Jamesian
domination theory, and it is only with the clearly Whartonian
studies of the 1970s—for example, Cynthia Wolff's *A Feast of
Words: The Triumph of Edith Wharton* (1977) and R.W.B. Lewis'
Edith Wharton: A Biography (1977)—that one sees Wharton "moving down from the literary attic—where she was relegated until
recently as a sort of Henry James in corsets—into the front
parlor" (Tyler 26).

The pessimism of Wharton's major works, many of which border on the naturalistic, gave rise to another form of prejudice, that related to the issue of class consciousness. Wharton did not have to wait until the radical 1930s to be attacked for her non-proletarian material. Early in the 1900s, she was criticized for her standing in the upper class. For example, Julia R. Tutwiler, in her 1903 "description" of Wharton, writes:

> For Mrs. Wharton belongs to that small and exclusive chapter of artists who have achieved without the accepted incentives to achievement. In one sense born to the place she has made her own in creative art, in another she has won it from the inaccessible seclusion of wealth and social position—she is wholly without the knowledge of life learned through study of the sordid and brutal face it turns upon those who struggle with "the meanness of opportunity" or are intimate with the clamoring needs of the body. (245)

Easily grafted onto this view is sexual prejudice, as can be seen in John Curtis Underwood's remarks on Wharton's "brilliancy":

> Brilliancy is a patrician quality, of the superficial, by the superficial, for the superficial. It is intrinsically alien to the genius of the Anglo-Saxon world, in particular to that of its male half; and the great mass of the world in general has some reason for looking at it with suspicion. (389–390)

In the 1930s, this view all but consigned Wharton to oblivion. V. L. Parrington called her a "temperamental aristocrat" (381), a conservative on the side of a "sterile world of class conventions and negations; a decadent Victorianism" (382). Granville Hicks cited her as a sort of genteel muckraker but, on the whole, Wharton's form and content were considered reactionary (here read both as politically wrong and aesthetically spurious), and she was ignored or "put in her place" by most radical critics. While by the late 1930s, this bias had become less pronounced, as late as the 1960s, one finds disguised but still operative attacks on her class status; as Patricia Plante warns in her 1962 "Edith

Wharton: A Prophet Without Due Honor," "it is an inverted form of snobbery to hold that truth can only be found among the poor and the under-privileged" (19). And one yet finds Wharton discussed as an anthropologist of a vanished era, a novelist of manners—that is, a snobbish social reporter for New York's 400—but little more.

The biases based on class or sex die hard in that they are perhaps more personal, more subjective, and also more deeply conditioned responses than later cultivated biases of aesthetic preferences. Edith Wharton was for critics and readers alike one of a new breed of American writers: she was a member of the affluent upper class as well as Scribner's chief moneymaker whose novels focused unremittingly upon dark visions of alienation and compromise. As John Harvey writes in "Contrasting Worlds: A Study in the Novels of Edith Wharton," "That a member of this inbred, over-civilized society should become a professional writer was in itself unusual, that a woman should do so was incredible" (190). Equally incredible was that Wharton could have been accepted widely as a great writer, regardless of her sex, by her contemporaries. The standard response up to the 1930s toward Wharton, as it was toward many women writers, is succinctly represented by Elizabeth A. Drew's piece, "Is There a 'Feminine' Fiction?" in which she writes:

when all is said, and in spite of the feminists with the queen bee in their bonnets, the fact remains that the creative genius of woman remains narrower than that of man, even in the novel. . . . In spite of equal education and equal opportunity, the scope of woman remains still smaller than the scope of man. (116)

Of course, as James intimated and Lubbock corroborated, Wharton was considered to have "a very feminine consciousness and a very masculine mind" (Lubbock 57). Wharton herself sensed such a split, perhaps intending not so much to comment on her particular gender construction but on the types of discourse then considered male and female. For instance, in her 1907 letter to Robert Grant, she writes, "I conceive my subjects like a man— that is, rather more architectonically & dramatically than most women—& then execute them like a woman; or rather, I sac-

rifice, to my desire for construction & breadth, the small inci-
dental effects that women have always excelled in, the episodical
characterisation, I mean" (*Letters* 124). One sees here her concern
over her inability to combine successfully both types of discourse,
in this particular instance to write a better novel than *The Fruit
of the Tree*. Her fiction was not, however, read by many as positive
attempts to unite male and female discourses. Instead, the concept of her bisexual mentality promoted by some critics led to
her being doubly attacked. She was criticized by many female
critics as being too cruel a writer, too masculine or inhumane,
versus, for example, Sarah Orne Jewett; male critics, in turn,
lambasted her for being "an elderly semi-male Minerva" (Underwood 351–352), an essentially "sexless" (Collins 54), here
read de-feminized or inhuman, writer. Wharton was more than
aware of this form of prejudice; though she often jokingly spoke
about herself as a self-made man, she requested that her private
papers remain sealed until 1968, " 'till,' she said, 'I shall be no
longer regarded as a woman but only as a writer in the long line
of writers' " (Kellogg 14). However, one particularly curious
form of critical analysis arose directly from Wharton's reticence
toward self-exposure: that is, critical interpretation based upon
psycho-biographical speculation. Through their psychoanalytic
analyses, critics have sometimes indirectly qualified Wharton's
aesthetic achievement by treating her work in the main as the
psychological working out of the traumas of childhood, feminine
sexual frustration, and extramarital dalliances and consequent
guilt. These psychological readings are curious in that they often
seek resolution to the traumas Wharton presents in her fiction
as not so easily resolvable. Edmund Wilson's "Justice to Edith
Wharton" (1938) most clearly opens this line of inquiry. More
sophisticated analysis of Wharton's art as compensation for lack
is available in Cynthia Wolff's major study, *A Feast of Words*, and
Wendy Gimbel's dissertation published in 1984 as *Edith Wharton:
Orphancy and Survival*. Such psychoanalytic readings will, no
doubt, be given further fuel by the recent publication of Wharton's letters.

Finally, some recent criticism recalls in a new way attention to
issues of gender, class, or cultural production. For instance, feminist studies, following upon, to be sure, the seminal work of

such critics as E. K. Brown, R.W.B. Lewis, Blake Nevius, and Geoffrey Walton, focus considerable attention on Wharton's accomplishment in light of the development of the American novel and of feminist discourse, the reception of American literature, and the promotion of social fiction. On the other hand, feminist criticism can also offer new trapdoors of misprision in its rationalization or condemnation of Wharton's supposed attitude toward women, an instance of forcing contemporary labels, here "feminist" or "anti-feminist," upon the material under investigation, labels that are not strictly applicable in either a historical or sociological sense. As Katherine Joslin remarks, "It would seem, at times, that critics, as well as readers, want a tragedy with a happy ending, complete with a strong heroine" (202); and several recent studies force such a reading of Wharton's overtly pessimistic fiction. In contrast to such criticism, Elizabeth Ammons' *Edith Wharton's Argument with America* offers highly critical and provocative analysis of Wharton's response to the "woman question." Taking off from a markedly different starting point, Judith Fryer's *Felicitous Space* revisions Wharton's fiction through considerations of the aesthetics of space, a radically new perspective from which to read her novels. Similarly, Dale Bauer's neo-Bakhtinian "The Failure of the Republic" in her *Feminist Dialogics* and Wai-chee Dimock's Marxist "Debasing Exchange" offer important new methods of reading *The House of Mirth*, ones which serve to elucidate Wharton's hierarchy of values rather than to render it even more incomprehensible or suspect.

Wharton's moral hierarchy is not particularly indecipherable, though it is, assuredly, far from simple. She, like Chopin, believed neither in absolute good nor in absolute evil. Repressive forces such as provincial, tribal society could offer the positive values of social continuity and security, while progressive forces such as the individualistic Lily Bart were subject to base materialistic motives. In that sense, Wharton's stance on the war of social forces, and on the longstanding relations between the sexes, was seemingly non-partisan. While it is true that Wharton was obviously pro-society—that is, society as she knew it at its best, as both genteel and highly moral—she was not one to disguise or to justify the degeneration of her society's morals and traditions. Indeed, she wrote to unmask just such iniquities.

Wharton viewed her own work as social fiction: "*No* novel worth anything can be anything but a novel 'with a purpose,' & if anyone who cared for the moral issue did not see in my work that *I* care for it, I should have no one to blame but myself—or at least my inadequate means of rendering my effects" (*Letters* 99). Her purpose is clearly seen in her mid-career works ranging from *The House of Mirth* to her last finished novel on Old New York, *The Age of Innocence*, as well as in her late dark visions. Despite her experimentation with technique, as in the Jamesian *The Reef* and the anti-pastoral *Ethan Frome*, her intention was constant: to analyze the causality of individual and collective alienation. She wrote continuously of societies that build prisons with traditions, applaud limited perceptions instead of a constant questioning of inherited values, and denounce social evolution while devolving themselves into a wasteland of lost hopes and living dead. Katherine Joslin argues that Wharton's "pessimism and sense of the inexplicable disarrangement of all we seek to order is modernist in impulse" (197). Wharton's is an essentially despairing world view, then, one shade darker than Chopin's bleak outlook. She lived long enough to feel not only the death of romanticism but also the anguish of modernity.

6

Edith Wharton's Social Fiction

Edith Wharton's fiction is more overtly reflective of reality and the confluence of reality and ideology than are Kate Chopin's psychological texts, but both individualize the general in order to offer clear examples of particular limits and defeat. The social world of Wharton's novels—from *The House of Mirth* through *The Age of Innocence* to *The Children* is Chopin's taken one temporal step further and relocated to the North or the Continent. It is a world wherein the old order is giving way to the new, one in which women have gained little and lost much despite the emergence of seemingly progressive social theories and practices.

Wharton's primary fictional world is specifically that of New York at home and abroad, that contemporaneous with her own life. Prior to 1870, New York was predominantly middle-class in tradition and manners (what most readers now qualitatively call upper-class in terms of quantitative wealth). However, in the 1870s, genteel society began to lose its social clout in the face of Big Business and frontier money, the frontier being literally everything west of the narrow East Coast. Infra-class struggle was openly fought in New York's opera houses, dining salons, and ballrooms between genteel and parvenu manners; less obvious but no less crucial was a subtler conflict between Wall Street and Fifth Avenue, two separate worlds for the genteel, one and the same for the new money class. Wharton's fiction chronicles the stages of this social war in which genteel society's rules of the game continually shift in order first to spurn, then to tame, and finally to assimilate new wealth into its coffers. In other words, Wharton focuses in the main specifically on her own genteel world disintegrating under pressure of the arrivistes, the modern world. She reconstructs that metamorphosis of her supposedly genteel world into a modern, seemingly barbaric society in that she both censures "genteel" society for its own rapacious materialism, for its willingness to sacrifice its own ethics and traditions for hard cash, as well as rebuking the new materialist society for its own perverse form of amorality. In all her fiction, the social use and prescribed roles of women act as a thermometer by which to measure the heat of the social battle and the changes in social consciousness. Wharton, of course, does not rest with symbolic use of women; instead, she also delimits the reality of women during this period, a time of social transformation and ideological mutation.

Wharton's earliest fiction thematically centers on woman as martyr and sets forth in very bold strokes the nineteenth-century variant of true womanhood ideology. The basic tenets of this doctrine, as previously discussed, were woman's mental, physical, and economic subordination to man, an accepted sexual double standard, and the concept of female spiritual and aesthetic superiority or, as Janet Flanner writes, "a hard hierarchy of male money, of female modesty and morals" (171). At the base of this ideology was the belief in woman as sacrificer. As Jean Turner succinctly puts it in her excellent dissertation on nineteenth-century ideology in Wharton's works, "a woman achieved fulfillment only through serving others" (57). One sees this idealization dramatized repeatedly in Wharton's first stories and novellas.

Post–1870 society merely reinterpreted these concepts in order to justify its more openly materialistic orientation. If women were both martyrs and purveyors or guardians of aesthetics, it takes only one more step for woman to sacrifice personhood, to objectify herself into a work of art, an acknowledged ideological prescription criticized severely and notably by Charlotte Perkins Gilman and Thorstein Veblen among other contemporary social critics. Money then replaces lineage as the standard of social status, and woman becomes the most powerful social asset, "the showpiece of American capitalism" (Turner 85), "an emblem of some man's power to waste—a measure of his competitive superiority over other men" (Morris 9). The true woman becomes, in other words, subject to and ultimate object of conspicuous consumption:

The speculative fortunes gained from the Industrial Revolution and from the Civil War thus fostered the development of possessive tastes. The ultimate possession, of course, became Galatea: the artfully trained woman, bereft of economic assets but possessed of the capacity for tastefully dispersing and displaying a man's wealth. (Montgomery 891–892)

This construct of woman as a form of social capital lies at the center of Wharton's *The House of Mirth* and various stories of that period.

The objectification of woman reveals, however, profound contradictions between moral theory and social practice, contradictions which foster further alienation of the individual from material actualities and self-fulfillment. The irreconcilable distance between theory and practice becomes horrifically obvious. For instance, the ethical standards of honor in business and private life are clearly nonoperative in a world in which women are to constitute themselves merely as walking art works seemingly unconcerned with their upkeep and wherein men are required as well to maintain a nominal separation of Wall Street from home on Fifth Avenue even though, as is more than evident, the practical enactment of ideological prescriptions necessitates money and the getting of more money. Bourgeois sexual and social practices begin to reveal a particularly virulent level of distortion and destructiveness which can no longer remain unchallenged. Olga de Valdivia points out the inherent consequences of such severe disparity between ethical theory and actuality:

But what happens when the society is not morally conscious, or even worse, when it is unconsciously immoral? If this be the case, the individual has to choose between the two ways: either to follow the line of least resistance and be drowned in the immorality of his age, or to fight against it and be drowned in a sea of incomprehension. (57)

Wharton's response to this was her novels of individual revolt against society—*Ethan Frome, Summer,* and *The Reef*—none of which takes place in New York proper, all of which speak of extreme forms of individual and collective alienation present in any social world based on a romantic and reactionary set of cultural and sexual imperatives.

Wharton next focuses upon an alternative to such nihilistic negation. One might say she had momentarily arrived at and passed through her fictional heart of darkness. She reinstates the theme of "social art as capital" (Turner 123) but now satirically portrays both men and women as social and financial entrepreneurs. Her wickedly caustic *The Custom of the Country* studies the birth of a rapacious society, headed by Undine Spragg and Elmer Moffatt, delivered out of the death throes of the genteel.

In 1920, Wharton produced what most critics believe to be her great American novel, *The Age of Innocence,* which spans several generations and various social worlds. Here, Wharton explores fully the transformations introduced in her earlier works and painfully attempts to reconcile the good from the past with the positive of the present modern world, imagining briefly an unchaotic future of individual and collective fulfillment and security. Her late novels offer in turn a devastating denial of all those dreams. Her work, then, begins with analyses of particular genteel forms of self-effacement, then discovers specific avenues for self-fulfillment, and finally culminates in visions of profound self-alienation. Wharton's last works position her characters dancing frantically on the edge of the abyss.

Wharton exposed in two of her earliest stories, "The Fullness of Life" (1893) and "The Lamp of Psyche" (1895), two forms of alienation—that between male and female nature and that between woman's social and spiritual duties—as ideological givens. She then addresses the possibility of reconciling opposites and determines at what cost that might be effected. In the first piece, a woman dies and is offered eternal happiness with her ideal mate, one whose nature will reflect her own perfectly. Her marriage has been a socially enviable but personally unfulfilling affair, and the woman realizes the cause of this as rooted in the ideological conditioning which demands limited, specific role-playing from both men and women and which also denies any possible satisfaction of woman's desire to know and to be known:

> But I have sometimes thought that a woman's nature is like a great house full of rooms: there is the hall, through which everyone passes in going in and out; the drawing room, where one receives formal visits; the sitting room, where the members of the family come and go as they list; but beyond that, far beyond, are other rooms, the handles of whose doors perhaps are never turned; no one knows the way to them, no one knows whither they lead; and in the innermost room, the holy of holies, the soul sits alone and waits for a footstep that never comes. (*Stories* I, 14)

One sees, then, from her first work Wharton's negative reading of separate spheres, envisioned here as the public one of society and family in which men position themselves versus the private one of spiritualized desire in which women remain desolately alone. Her character's husband remains cloddishly oblivious to his wife's inner nature; she dies hearing not the footstep of a lover but "the creaking of her husband's boots—those horrible boots" (12). The later story begins with the opposite premise, that a wife and husband have "seen each other's souls" (42) but then goes on to offer another deconstruction of man's nature from a woman's point of view, an unmasking of the seemingly perfect lover by a modern-day Psyche. Her interpretation follows fast upon discovery of an unmanly and therefore morally reprehensible act in her husband's past:

> Formerly he had been to her like an unexplored country, full of bewitching surprises and recurrent revelations of wonder and beauty; now she had measured and mapped him, and knew beforehand the direction of every path she trod. His answer to her question had given her the clue to the labyrinth; knowing what he had once done, it seemed quite simple to forecast his future conduct. (57)

Once more woman's consciousness seems superior to man's circumscribable and earthbound mentality, her sense of morality superior to his potentially base pragmatism. In both cases, however, and despite the patently irreconcilable natures of the partners, the women compromise themselves and, one might argue, their spirituality by choosing to remain with their husbands. The wife in "The Fullness of Life" believes she must do so, since she claims to have no choice in the matter. Because her husband loves her, in his own boorish way, and considers her his soulmate, her duty is to abjure the fullness of life for eternity and to wait for him and the creaking of his boots. Her loss is of "no matter," she says: "I shall be the only sufferer, for he always thought that he understood me" (19). She thus reinstates the separation of spheres she so detested before. Similarly, the wife in "The Lamp of Psyche," a not very pretty woman past thirty, begs forgiveness for calling down judgment upon her husband. She does so because she is "a woman of sense" and, perhaps, also as her punishment for having loved desire too well (57). Wharton thus early on calls into question the nineteenth-century concepts of woman as aesthetic and moral superior to man as well as the value of woman's self-effacement as willing martyr to social duty: each of her female characters does not so much do the right thing as merely the expected, each at great cost to herself.

These themes are recast in "Friends" (1900) which relates the aftereffects of Penelope Bent's ignominious return home after abandonment by her fiancé. Her teaching position, the one genteel career open to her, has in the meantime been awarded to her less qualified but poverty-stricken girlfriend. In this case, after much bathetic breastbeating, Penelope decides to disguise her own financial and personal needs in order to persuade her friend to keep the job:

The experience of the last weeks had flung her out of her orbit, whirling her through spaces of moral darkness and bewilderment. She seemed to have lost her connection with the general scheme of things, to have no further part in the fulfillment of the laws that made life comprehensible and duty a joyful impulse. Now the old sense of security had returned. There still loomed before her, in tragic amplitude, the wreck of her individual hope; but she had escaped from the falling ruins and stood safe, outside of herself, in touch once more with the common troubles of her kind, enfranchised forever from the bondage of a lonely grief. (I, 214)

Here, sacrifice seen as abnegation of female individual will for the sake of "her kind," a renunciation of one's desire for self-fulfillment, is equated with moral rectitude, mental and social security, and salvation from individual alienation.

Combining the themes of these stories, Wharton's two early novellas—*The Touchstone* (1900) and *Sanctuary* (1903)—focus obsessively on problematic differences between male and female consciousnesses but the absolute social necessity of woman's role as moral guardian. It is particularly ironic, however, that in these two works the sacrifice or subjugation of female will and desire is done so not for the sake of "her kind" but to enable male self-fulfillment.

In *The Touchstone*, Stephen Glennard finances his marriage to Alexa Trent through the sale of personal letters written to him by a famous woman author who loved him. By doing so, Glennard ostensibly compromises the social or patriarchal code of honor and is consequently consumed by self-hatred. Alexa, with her "intuitive feminine justness" (12) rescues him; her moral superiority enables her to comprehend and to accept his past actions and, further, to devise some sort of mental and material penance which will exonerate him of his sins. Alexa, then, stands by her corrupted man and, finally, through a sharing of his penance, raises him to her morally purer level.

So too in *Sanctuary* does a woman offer herself as sacrificial lamb in atonement for a man's wrongdoing, a plot recalling much sentimental Victorian domestic fiction which centers on the relationship between mother and child. Kate Orme discovers her fiancé has unethically acquired his inherited fortune, his actions literally costing two lives. Her initial response to this scandal parallels Penelope Bent's mental travail on her own dilemma:

Her survey of life had always been marked by the tendency to seek out ultimate relations, to extend her researches to the limit of her imaginative experience. But hitherto she had been like some young captive brought up in a windowless palace whose painted walls she takes for the actual world. Now the palace had been shaken to its base, and through a cleft in the walls she looked out upon life. For the first moment all was indistinguishable blackness; then she began to detect vague shapes and confused gestures in the depths. There were people below there, men like Denis, girls like herself—for under the unlikeness she felt the strange affinity—all struggling in that awful coil of moral darkness, with agonized hands reaching up for rescue. Her heart shrank from the horror of it, and then in a passion of pity, drew back to the edge of the abyss. (22–23)

Kate's impulse is to break with Denis, an act which would both reveal and protect her purer moral nature. Yet, after a scene with her fiancé's mother and a talk with her father, she awakens to her proper, if almost unbelievable, role in terms of ideological expectations. Kate comes to believe, despite her vision of engulfing "moral darkness," that collectivity transcends individuality, that society's immorality requires not censure but self-sacrifice:

She had begun to perceive that the fair surface of life was honeycombed by a vast system of moral sewage. Every respectable household had its special arrangements for the private disposal of family secrets; it was only among the reckless and improvident that such hygienic precautions were neglected. Who was she to pass judgment on the merits of such a system? The social health must be preserved: the means devised were the results of long experience and the collective instinct of self-preservation. (60–61)

By a stunning display of ratiocination, Kate decides that her moral superiority is "a rampart to lean on" (26) above the sewers, and Kate willingly takes up her position as moral sentry: she sacrifices her individuality, in a "mystic climax of effacement" (67), by taking on the role of moral guardian to Denis' future child. That her martyrdom is of value is proven in the second half of the book. Despite the temptations of an opportunistic new woman, an alien presence in the society of two in which Kate has invested herself, Kate's son chooses personal honor over public material success: that is, he proves himself free of the sins of his father by emulating the virtues of his mother. He loses his woman but finds sanctuary with his mother. Whereas in *The Touchstone*, Glennard fell upon Alexa's breast in relief at the end, here Kate rejoices that "all at once she had him in her breast as in a shelter" (180). In both novellas, then, women's exceptional self-sacrifice sustains the society approved of by mothers, however immoral that society might be as a rule. Kate can believe in the end that her actions have made her son into a good man; she saves him from the abyss into which had he fallen, he "should never have come up again alive" (184).

The above works are patently melodramatic, both in plot and in their argument that compromise of the female self for the sake of male salvation always results in fantastical happy endings. They are also disquieting works in the double vision they proffer: woman as healing angel but an angel consigned to the Herculean task of cleaning out society's sewers or, worse yet, of merely concealing the moral abyss from view. Indeed, in these works Wharton herself conceals and implicitly denies the fact that the willing submission of woman to family and society, woman's complicity with the hegemony, has an equal potential for tragic resolution. Wharton later admitted that she felt the first two stories were "written 'at the top of my voice,' & The Fulness [sic] of Life is one long shriek" (*Letters* 36); and it is a great temptation to write off these early works and the contradictions therein as first failed attempts at realism. Yet, one can also argue that Wharton had already found her voice, and other works of the same period offer a somewhat muted, more analytical variant of that original double vision. Her excellent satire "The Pelican" (1899) points out that personal sacrifice for others might be materially necessary at times but beyond that, taken up as a way of life, can become both unethical and pathetic. Further, in "A Cup of Cold Water" (1899), the male protagonist speculates that the moral code which justifies such sacrifice is a complete sham:

Was not all morality based on a convention? What was the staunchest code of ethics but a trunk with a series of false bottoms? Now and then one had the illusion of getting down to absolute right or wrong, but it was only a false bottom—a removable hypothesis—with another false bottom beneath. There is no getting beyond the relative. (I, 157–158)

Despite his consciousness of ethical relativity, he submits himself to society's punishment for his admittedly illegal actions; he also counsels a woman to humble herself before her husband and his family in order to be reinstated into their society. However, in that same volume, *The Greater Inclination,* Wharton included "The Muse's Tragedy" (1989) which poignantly delimits the value of the martyr's life, arguing that capitulation to the relative does indeed matter a good deal. After experiencing an ecstatic relationship with a man, the heroine sees her previous life of sacrifice as sterile waste: she says that his love for her "has shown me, for the first time, all that I have missed" (78). Similarly, in "The Quicksand" (1904), Wharton explores another obsessive mother-son relationship. Here, however, the mother's sacrifice for her son has no positive results. In fact, in the end she convinces her son's fiancée to abjure a life of sacrifice by leaving him. The moral of this story is clear: the attempt to rescue an unethical life through self-sacrifice leads only to a life of self-alienation and self-compromise for all concerned. And one might even question *The Sanctuary*'s happy ending in that the relationship between mother and son seems not so much in the end a celebration of moral truth as it is a regressive state of mutual dependency which severely limits both characters' effecting a relationship to their world.

Wharton's most detailed analysis and rejection of the martyr's consciousness is seen in her *The Bunner Sisters*, written in 1892 but left unpublished until 1916, a novella that is Wharton's only extended study of lower working class life. It analyzes another society of two threatened by an outsider, here the relationship between two repressed sisters who become enamored with the same man. The story both dramatizes the conflicts in such a love triangle as well as focusing upon Ann Eliza's sacrifices for her younger sister Evelina, these sacrifices ranging in degree from offering Evelina the larger portion of pie at dinner to giving up her only suitor. Both sisters suffer from psychological and financial deprivation; at the outset of the book, both clearly desire escape from the impoverished "monastic" confines of their hat shop (*Xingu* 320). Ann Eliza meets Herman Ramy when she buys Evelina a birthday present, and he quickly becomes an integral but disruptive part of their lives in that the sisters become competitors for his attention. However, perhaps as atonement for having wanted him for herself, for having experienced desire, Ann Eliza consciously chooses self-effacement, taking up the role of martyr for the sake of her sister's well-being. When Ramy unexpectedly proposes to Ann Eliza instead of the more feminine Evelina, Ann Eliza gives him up, for "she was well-trained in the arts of renunciation" (330). She does so only to push

Ramy toward Evelina, and she finds solace in such supreme self-sacrifice: "She knew the crucial moment of her life had passed, and she was glad that she had not fallen below her own ideal" (369). She does not realize until too late that her ideals are derived from a code of ethics that is itself highly suspect or that the putting into practice of such a code is far from saintly, that her motives might by closer to the masochistic maternalism enacted by Wharton's other martyr-women.

Indeed, self-renunciation does not automatically effect self-fulfillment for others. Ann Eliza loses contact with Evelina and discovers, in her search for her sister, that Ramy is a drug addict. Not surprisingly, Evelina's marriage to him proves a bitter failure, and he abandons her after the death of their day-old baby. Evelina then returns home mortally ill. Ann Eliza realizes in turn how "sick" she has been, how perverse her actions:

For the first time in her life she dimly faced the awful problem of the inutility of self-sacrifice. Hitherto she had never thought of questioning the inherited principles which had guided her life. Self-effacement for the good of others had always seemed to her both natural and necessary; but then she had taken it for granted that it implied the securing of that good. Now she perceived that to refuse the gifts of life does not insure their transmission to those for whom they have been surrendered; and her familiar heaven was unpeopled. She felt she could no longer trust in the goodness of God, and that if he was not good he was not God, and there was only a black abyss above the roof of Bunner Sisters. (420–421)

Almost as if in punishment, as a fitting end, for self-effacement, Ann Eliza loses the shop after having paid for her sister's marriage, illness, and funeral. Rather than drifting "down the stream of Life unfettered and serene as a Summer cloud," Ann Eliza instead descends in the end into "the abyss of soullessness" (386–387). Thus the concept of woman as willing martyr is proven in this case to be destructive in the extreme, killing both the supposed receiver of the martyr's self-offering and the future children who were meant to profit from that sacrifice. Further, while society indoctrinates its sacrificial lambs in the maintenance of hegemonic codes, it offers little compensation or consolation for sacrifices that prove socially negligible, here those of a working class woman done for another working class woman, a sister, "her kind." At the conclusion, Ann Eliza walks the streets searching for a position, her past and future negated, speechless.

Wharton, then, from the outset of her career intuited that her society's code of ethics is not a rampart protecting one from seemingly indescribable moral and social chaos nor, as Ann Eliza imagines with her limited consciousness, is its immorality beyond the comprehension of the individual. Instead, Wharton suggests repeatedly, even in these her melodramatic early works, that society has accommodated unethical compromises and practices through its promotion of specific ideological theories, particularly in its glorification of the woman martyr, and that by virtue of their acceptance of society's values each of its collective members thus conceals a heart of darkness within. The question for Wharton then becomes how one is to exorcise that darkness without tearing out the heart.

A less abysmal but complementary view is presented in "Souls Belated" (1899), another early work which introduces a drama Wharton will continually restage throughout her career, notably in *The Age of Innocence*. In this piece, a woman leaves her husband for the man she admires and loves, an artist who stands in sharp contrast to the rich boor she married. Lydia's elopement with Ralph Gannett constitutes her revolt against what she sees as conventional morality and begins her struggle to maintain her outlaw ethics of individual freedom. She tells Ralph, "Of course one acts as one can—as one must perhaps—pulled by all sorts of invisible threads; but at least one needn't pretend, for social advantages, to subscribe to a creed that ignores the complexity of human motives—that classifies people by arbitrary signs . . ." (I, 110–111). However, as the events in the story prove, she has not fully understood the resiliency of those invisible threads to theoretical self-detachment. When Lydia's case is reflected back to her by Mrs. Cope, another married woman who has eloped with a much younger man, she is appalled. She realizes then her utter conventionality and her need for social position and approval. It is not surprising that she fails in her last attempt at self-constitution as outlaw, that she surrenders to self-accommodation by returning to Ralph whom she will then no doubt marry. As Ralph tells Lydia concerning social conventions,

" 'One may believe in them or not; but as long as they do rule the world it is only by taking advantage of their protection that one can find a *modus vivendi*' " (111). They must, in other words, give in to convention and admit to their self-identification with an immoral society if they are to live as they have been brought up to expect. At the end they are "bound together" not "in a *noyade* of passion" but in a noyade of self-compromise (125). They are at the close outlaws of passion become social puppets "mechanically" manipulated by those same invisible threads Lydia so wished to sever (126).

Wharton's intense and detailed critical analyses of a morally disintegrating or, as R.W.B. Lewis posits, a reintegrating society properly begin with *The House of Mirth* (1905) and include all major works thereafter. The martyrdom paradigm led her quickly to a critical and literary dead end; Wharton perhaps saw her reading therein of ideology as too strident or simplistic. Wharton now turned for her subject matter to the more complex construct of woman as social capital.

As set out in the opening section of this chapter, the role of woman as social capital superceded by incorporation the more traditional one of woman as martyr, and even in some of the early works, notably *The Touchstone*, Wharton plays with men's reading of woman as "public property" (48). In that novella, Glennard at first rationalizes his use of Aubyn's letters by translating the problematic intimate relations between them into the depersonalized language of economics: "But in the dissolution of sentimental partnerships it is seldom that both associates are able to withdraw their funds at the same time; and Glennard gradually learned that he stood for the venture on which Mrs. Aubyn had irretrievably staked her all. It was not the kind of figure he cared to cut" (21–22). He also believes himself in love with another woman, though the reader might be wont to view this relationship simply as a less unappealing self-reflection: "if man is at times indirectly flattered by the moral superiority of woman, her mental ascendancy is extenuated by no such oblique tribute to his powers. The attitude of looking up is a strain on the muscles; and it was becoming more and more Glennard's opinion that brains, in a woman, should be merely the obverse of beauty" (18–19). Alexa Trent is in the second half of the

novella his beautiful guardian angel, their penitential relationship secured by his having made an immense profit on the "sure
thing" (34) of selling Aubyn's letters so that he might marry
Alexa, might "get into a big thing, and without appreciable risk"
(47). While that novella ends happily for the lovers since they
suffer and atone for Glennard's actions, their newfound dependency on one another remains curiously dissatisfying, perhaps because it is predicated upon the selling out of another
woman, the making of her private self into public property. As
Glennard admits about his treatment of Aubyn, "I took everything from her, I deceived her, I despoiled her, I destroyed her"
(156). Alexa's response that he paid Aubyn back by allowing her
"the happiness of giving" (156) obfuscates the issue by implying
that man's acting upon passive women is indistinguishable from
women's desire. Glennard despairs that he cannot because of his
actions escape from Aubyn, that "it was as though he had married her instead of the other" and that "she had gained her point
at last" (59). Alexa also declares that "She's made you into the
man she loved" (156). One assumes, however, that Glennard will
also choose to believe Alexa's argument that this figure is now
one he should like to cut. In this way the subtext of a woman's
revenge is erased and done so by her rival. *The Touchstone*'s ending, then, foreshadows that of *The House of Mirth* for Selden as
does its focus on the sacrifice of women, here both lover and
wife, to male desire and male self-constitution.

Similarly, several of Wharton's early stories point to the concept of marriage as business, men as dealers in the property of
women, as well as the conventional belief that a man's status is
reflected by the appearance and manner of his wife and material
possessions. For example, the satiric "The Line of Least Resistance" (1900) recounts the acknowledged domination of a rich
man by his wife as well as his compromised ethics when he
discovers and finally conceals her unfaithfulness to him. The tale
clearly shows that the husband's social consciousness relies upon,
in that it is reflected, by his mirror-image mate and that the loss
of self-esteem is less cataclysmic than the ruination of social re-
gard, a public losing of face. Even more cynical is "The Other
Two" (1904) which exposes a husband's attitude toward his twice-
divorced wife, Alice. Waythorn is continually and disconcertingly

thrust into the company of the other two husbands. At first, he mentally belittles his wife for too openly appearing as used goods:

She was "as easy as an old shoe"—a shoe that too many feet had worn. Her elasticity was the result of tension in too many different directions. Alice Haskett—Alice Varick—Alice Waythorn—she had been each in turn, and had left hanging to each name a little of her privacy, a little of her personality, a little of the inmost self where the unknown god abides.... With grim irony Waythorn compared himself to a member of a syndicate. He held so many shares in his wife's personality and his predecessors were his partners in the business. (393)

At the conclusion, however, Waythorn has managed to rationalize a means of profit-making from his partners' work:

He even began to reckon up the advantages which accrued from it, to ask himself if it were not better to own a third of a wife who knew how to make a man happy than a whole one who had lacked opportunity to acquire the art. For it *was* an art, and made up, like all others, of concessions, eliminations and embellishments; of light judiciously thrown and shadows skillfully softened. (394)

This theme of woman objectified through her social art as capital stands at the center of *The House of Mirth*, and it is in this work that Wharton reveals in detail the "concessions, eliminations and embellishments" necessary for both profitable self-capitalization and effective social survival.

The House of Mirth, originally entitled "A Moment's Ornament" and then "The Year of the Rose," recounts the social decline and final annihilation of Lily Bart. It is, as Louis Auchincloss writes, "the drama of the hunt of a beautiful and desperate creature by a pack of remorseless hounds" ("Afterword" 346) in which both hunters and hunter are complicit. The novel portrays the old money class of the 1900s wherein, as Louis Kronenberger notes, "society itself, though distinct inroads have been made on the correctness of its manners and the roster of its memberships, is still an identifiable and despotic collective force, not only for those waiting to get in or being shown the way out, but even for those who are at home in its drawing rooms" (255–256). Even

though this society appears to be still genteel and morally stead-
fast, it is in reality one corrupted through its basic materialist
orientation and its attempted assimilation of the morally suspect
new money class. *The House of Mirth* is in essence a bitter cataloguing of monetary and human values. Herein, social status
and moral integrity are determined by wealth and, as Marie
Bristol writes, "society people use each other constantly; the
women use the men for money, the men use the women for
sexual and display purposes" (373). Wai-chee Dimock in her
"Debasing Exchange" elaborates in great detail "the power of
the marketplace . . . to reproduce itself, in its ability to assimilate
everything else into its domain. As a controlling logic, a mode
of human conduct and human association, the marketplace is
everywhere, ubiquitous and invisible. Under its shadow even the
more private affairs take on the essence of business transactions,
for the realm of human relations is fully contained within an all-
encompassing business ethic" (783). *The House of Mirth* severely
criticizes such a society that favors depersonalization, manipulation of the vulnerable for the profit of the secure, the limited
and limiting consciousness of the collective over the potential
and awakened consciousness of rare individuals. The novel also
attests to Wharton's understanding both of "the dynamics of
capitalist *production*" as well as of "the corruptions and insecurities of capitalist *exchange*" (Coontz 212). Wharton speaks of these
issues through her analysis of Lily Bart's conditioned feminine
role-playing and of society's judgment on her as this is reflected
through male characters.

One learns quickly that Lily Bart was born into genteel society
and inculcated with its ideology of true womanhood. She defines
her social self as that of a beautiful object to be bought and
maintained by the highest bidder and, at moments of extreme
stress, her language or thoughts reflect a deterministic rhetoric
justifying her determinedly limited social consciousness:

Inherited tendencies had combined with early training to make her the
highly specialized product she was: an organism as helpless out of its
narrow range as the sea-anemone torn from the rock. She had been
fashioned to adorn and delight; to what other end does nature round
the rose-leaf and paint the humming-bird's breast? And was it her fault

that the purely decorative mission is less easily and harmoniously fulfilled among social beings than in the world of nature? That it is apt
to be hampered by material necessities or complicated by moral scru-
ples? (486-487)

Even though she is willfully caught up in her society's constant
trafficking in women, Lily's search for a buyer is a desperate
one. Her family was financially ruined when she was nineteen,
thus materially forcing her out of a major trading position and
into a buyer's market. At twenty-nine, her value as a beautiful
object is fast diminishing, and the spectre of the "dingy" life of
genteel poverty is anathema to her. Her goal is "to go into partnership" (18), to find a husband for whom she can act as "the
one possession in which he took sufficient pride to spend money
on it" (78). However, inherently incompatible with her social
sense of self as capital is her personal sense of self as pure moral
and spiritual being. These clashing consciousnesses, duelling
concepts within one socio-sexual ideology, alienate Lily first from
herself and eventually from her collective. She cannot morally
play her social role to the hilt; neither can she completely give
up the game and find solace in her womanhood ideals. Ultimately, for Lily, the resolution to her dilemma is movement out
of a world wherein "all the men and women she knew were like
atoms whirling away from each other in some wild centrifugal
dance" (516) and into "the dim abysses of unconsciousness"
(521). Unlike Edna Pontellier, she does not experience a positive
awakening of self: Lily only learns what she is not and what she
cannot be.

Lily's social decline, from upper middle-class status down
through the parvenus to the working class, occurs both as the
cause of and as her response to various relationships she has
with men. These relationships prove continually ineffective as a
means of social salvation since they too reflect the alienating
consciousnesses present in Lily herself. For example, Simon
Rosedale, a new money Jew, perceives Lily primarily as social
capital necessary for his acceptance into Fifth Avenue society:
"it was becoming more and more clear to him that Miss Bart
herself possessed precisely the complementary qualities needed
to round off his social personality" (195). He proposes marriage

to her in terms of a business deal fully aware of the fact that she finds him personally repulsive and socially suspect. Lily, however, chooses at this point not to compromise her moral self by marrying for money. Ironically, when the time comes that she is willing to sacrifice her personal ethics for the security of Rosedale's partnership, her exchange value as capital has so diminished that Rosedale will not then compromise himself in order to save her.

Similarly, Lily mismanages her business relationship with Gus Trenor, a wealthy and married member of established society. Lily acts out the role of helpless female for Trenor and, in effect, sells her social favors for money. Lily, however, denies the sexual aspects implicit in the bargain, rejecting Trenor's money only after discovering its actual wage nature, when Trenor exacts immediate payment. Lily manages to escape with her social and moral selves intact, if slightly besmirched; the experience, nevertheless, awakens her consciousness of society's immorality: "She was realizing for the first time that a woman's dignity may cost more to keep up than her carriage; and that the maintenance of a moral attitude should be dependent on dollars and cents, made the world appear a more sordid place than she had conceived it" (273).

Her relationship with George Dorset is equally unsatisfying, and her dependence on his adulterous wife, Bertha, is patently self-destructive. Early on in the story, Lily comes into possession of Bertha's love letters to Lawrence Selden. Despite this proof that Bertha is morally corrupt, Lily maintains her friendship with Bertha for the sake of social security. In return, Lily's value for Bertha is that of a shield for her illicit activities; beyond that public arrangement, no private affection or sense of loyalty is shared, for, as Judith Fetterley points out, "relationships between 'beautiful objects' are hostile and competitive rather than supportive" ("Temptation" 203). Again, when scandal rears its head, it is Lily who is compromised. George tacitly offers himself to her if Lily will proffer in turn proof of Bertha's infidelity. Yet again, Lily cannot do so as that act stands against her womanhood ideals. Bertha, a socially secure married woman, can then attack Lily's precarious public self by implicitly accusing her of her own crime, adultery. Appearances triumph over reality, the social collective over the individual, leaving Lily "poised on the brink of a chasm with one graceful foot advanced to assert her unconsciousness that the ground was failing her" (309). Finally, Lily cannot justify blackmailing Bertha, despite the social degradation forced on her by Bertha, even though this act would directly result in Lily's marriage to Rosedale and consequent social and financial security. Once more Lily cannot sanction immoral acts; however, neither can she steer clear of them since she must live within society.

Most perplexing and ultimately destructive is Lily's relationship with Lawrence Selden, the one man she supposedly truly loves. Lily is attracted to him because he seems to see through her social presentation of self and thus he appeals to her hidden vision of self-possibility:

How alluring the world outside the cage appeared to Lily, as she heard its door clang on her! In reality, as she knew, the door never clanged: it stood always open; but most of the captives were like flies in a bottle, and having once flown in, could never regain their freedom. It was Selden's distinction that he had never forgotten the way out. (86–87)

Like the free animal in Chopin's "Emancipation," Selden seems above Lily's sordid social world, and, in addition, he professes a radically new code of ethics that complements Lily's own moral sense as well as her desire for delivery from social estrangement and self-alienation: " 'My idea of success,' he said, 'is personal freedom.'...'From everything—from money, from poverty, from ease and anxiety, from all the material accidents. To keep a kind of republic of the spirit—that's what I call success' " (108). What Lily chooses not to perceive is that Selden can afford to pose as social critic and rebel because he is, despite his financial situation, firmly entrenched within that society. The only difference between Selden and Lily's other men is that Selden's instinct for possession is coupled with romantic ideals. This is made more than evident if one contrasts Selden's private sentiments about Lily to his public pronouncements and actions, the former vacuous—as his republic of the spirit is a social void— and the latter characterized by the utter irresponsibility justified by his limited social consciousness which is that of the collective.

Selden initially relates only to Lily's social self, to Lily as beautiful object, and in important ways never wavers from this position as her distant appreciator. This attitude effectively absolves him of responsibility toward her; he can counsel her on the necessity of using her social art at the cost of her ethics— " 'Ah, well, there must be plenty of capital on the look-out for such an investment!' " (18)—while making clear that he cannot fit the bill and will not foot the bill. However, when Lily openly uses her social arts or is manipulated as capital, Selden turns about-face, criticizes, and abandons her, for he can conceal from himself his own inadequacies only by damning her for her inability to live out their moral pact, one which he initiates but which, again, costs him nothing. In addition, she cannot then enter into his republic of the spirit, both because she and it are false, nor will he assist her in the realization of their moral ideal; as Selden says of his republic, " 'it's a country one has to find the way to one's self' " (108). Selden, in effect, wants Lily to fulfill the concepts of true womanhood ideology most complementary to himself. He expects Lily, despite her precarious social and financial situation, to prove herself a worthy mirror of his idealism: "His craving was for the companionship of one whose point of view should justify his own, who should confirm, by deliberate observation, the truth to which his intuitions had leaped" (247). Lily thus has a value for Selden too, and it is one that cannot be capitalized upon without profound compromises on her part. In *The House of Mirth*, the beautiful object always pays.

At the end of the book, Lily's awakened social consciousness pointedly questions her society and its system of ethics. In a bleak vision, Lily comprehends that her humanity was of little value in an inhumane world and that her moral conscience proved of little use to her against the alienating experience of life within an impersonal, mechanistic society wherein the "I" becomes only a "one":

"I have tried hard—but life is difficult, and I am a very useless person. I can hardly be said to have an independent existence. I was just a screw or a cog in the great machine I called life, and when I dropped out of it I found I was of no use anywhere else. What can one do when one finds that one only fits into one hole? One must get back to it, or be thrown out into the rubbish heap." (498)

Lily cannot, then, live in a morally corrupt and corrupting society, recreate herself as a social puppet, nor can she live outside of society—for example, in Selden's republic—since that is a negation of reality. Neither can she find a place in another social class; her conditioning makes her helpless outside the doors of her cage. Lily can, in other words, question and reject the limited social consciousness she has disclosed, but she cannot find a positive alternative to it:

That was the feeling which possessed her now—the feeling of being something rootless and ephemeral, mere spin-drift of the whirling surface of existence, without anything to which the poor little tentacles of self could cling before the awful flood submerged them. And as she looked back she saw that there had never been a time when she had had any real relation to life. (515–516)

Lily does have one brief encounter with a potentially humane and humanistic community when she visits Nellie Struthers and her child. However, this one glimpse into what the reader sees is a patently pastoral vision of working-class life cannot halt Lily's final radical self-effacement. Nellie's world is yet again one into which Lily cannot enter: it is as socially unreal to her as is Selden's republic. Instead, she surrenders herself to the only world in which her self-will and desire can be fulfilled, a dream state into which she wanders, clutching to herself the only ideals left to her, spiritual and maternal love. She lives out at last the fantasy suggested in her grey letter seal—"*Beyond!* beneath a flying ship" (249)—amid the dingy surroundings she once so feared. She dies "estranged," unrecognizable as "her real self," "unrecognizing" (526); and in the end, the tragedy of her death is as easily rationalized as was the tragedy of her life by those left behind. Just as Selden appreciated her beauty in her tableau vivant, he finds inexpressible value for his sense of self as lover and beloved in her tableau mort.

Wharton herein bitterly indicts society for its willful destruction of those who constitute its body, censuring individuals, including Lily herself, for upholding, however passively, a degenerate and hypocritical social and moral code. Wharton shows it is a step toward a revitalized consciousness to question the social imperatives but that one must also be able to ask the right questions in time and to translate the answers into practice, toward the realization of a positive alternative collective view. It is true that Lily's awakened social consciousness is forced upon her by the contingencies of her life and that she was, at the outset of the novel, near social death, but her particular physical demise was not inevitably predetermined. Her death is unnatural, directly caused by the clash of consciousnesses within her; her ability to transform her critical knowledge into pragmatic action proves nonexistent. More important, however, than Wharton's portrayal of one particular case, the life and death of a Lily Bart, is that *The House of Mirth* stands as Wharton's first extended analysis of society revealed as a sterile world of vicious fools. As Wai-chee Dimock argues, Lily's world is a "detestable and inevitable" "totalizing system" which hoards its emotional capital (783) yet exacts the highest cost of living from those least able to pay. The tragedy is not that Lily dies but that society goes on untouched by the rise and fall of one of its daughters.

Wharton's work up to this point was clearly moving toward a rejection of nineteenth-century social consciousness and its questionable system of ethics. If the constructs within the ideology of true womanhood could be proven to be stultifying and ultimately destructive for both men and women, it was only a further step in social analysis to see that the society that fostered that ideology must be radically transformed. Wharton's first response to her own awakened social consciousness was, in many ways, as fatalistic as that of Lily Bart or Edna Pontellier. Her novels of individual revolt—*Ethan Frome, Summer,* and *The Reef*—are tragedies of social and moral desolation and isolation, all physically removed from Wharton's society but morally speaking about and to that same world.

The theme of individual revolt is not, of course, new to Wharton's work. Indeed, her first published story, "Mrs. Manstey's View" (1891), sets that motif in motion. In this piece, an elderly invalid, a lady fallen on hard times, has only one consolation in an otherwise meager life: a room with a view. When the neighboring landlady's extension of property threatens to erase that view, Mrs. Manstey rises from her sick bed and perpetrates very unladylike violence. She attempts to burn down the new building. Watching the flames, she contracts a cold and then dies of pneumonia. The story argues that one must fight to maintain one's horizons even if one kills oneself doing so, yet it is also clear that Mrs. Manstey's is a bittersweet and brief victory.

Wharton's *The Fruit of the Tree*, published two years after *The House of Mirth*, also details the necessity of individual revolt against the system, that which denies a room with a view to each member of society. In striking fashion, it recombines the issues introduced in earlier works: the destructive power of a frivolous society, the negative effects of women's self-martyrdom, the self-effacement required of women by men. The novel incorporates these concerns within its social problem plot, focusing as it does on the need for drastic reform in the relationships obtaining between employers and workers, between the ruling class, which lives luxuriously upon the profits from its factories, and the working class, the hard labor of which translates into those profits. *The Fruit of the Tree* is striking in that its argument seems a highly radical one for Wharton to make; she was, after all, not a woman of the factories. It is not, however, a particularly satisfying novel in that, like Chopin's *At Fault*, it focuses less on its supposedly central social problem, that of the need for socialist reform and, later, the morality of euthanasia, than on the difficulties men and women encounter loving one another, those difficulties arising, in this case, from gender and class expectations. In other words, the novel attempts too much in its attention to issues both of class and gender, yet it is important precisely because of that double critique.

The novel's central figure is John Amherst, son of a lady, who has aligned himself totally with the worker's cause. His radical politics eventually lead to his loss of position as assistant manager in the Westmore mills. Before he loses that job, he meets the widow of the factory's primary owner. She awakens him in several ways, appealing as she does both to his sexual desire as well as his desire to reexperience the beautiful life available to that class into which he was born. He quickly discounts both urges, rationalizing instead the social good they could do were they to join his politics with her material power. He sees in her, then, his ideological mate, and here ideology takes on double meaning: he assumes she will both share his politics and serve as his angel of the mills, that she will marry his cause when she unites with him but that she will also efface herself in him: "*He for God only, she for God in him*" (179). He proposes to her after an exhilarating sled ride, and they do marry. He learns, however, very quickly the risks deluded dreamers take when they "scramble into the chariot of the gods and try to do the driving" (162), a lesson which Wharton will reimagine in darker shades in her next work, *Ethan Frome*. Bessy proves to be uninterested in his "business" (192) and then becomes intractable when it comes to the question of her money being used to promote his reforms which seem totally unprofitable to her. Ironically, in her responses Bessy reveals herself as a true woman of the upper class: she upholds the tradition of separate spheres for men and women just as she demands to be maintained in the manner to which she is accustomed. She also has a very strong class consciousness indeed, but it is one that stands diametrically opposed to that of Amherst. Similarly, her gender consciousness determined as it is by her class allegiance conflicts with his gender expectations in that she has been raised to be a beautiful object but not the self-sacrificing angel he desires if that selflessness be at the cost of luxuriant self-objectification. In Bessy, Wharton reveals just how destructive such a true woman in a frivolous society can be: she collaborates in the oppression of an entire class of people and chooses to remain oblivious to this fact. Bessy, too, wants her room with a view, no matter what the cost to others. Yet, she is also profoundly dependent, unself-conscious; she is, as an older woman in her circle remarks, "one of the most harrowing victims of the plan of bringing up our girls in the double bondage of expediency and unreality, corrupting their bodies with luxury and their brains with sentiment, and leaving them to reconcile the two as best they can, or lose their souls in the attempt" (281). Understood in these terms, she is another Lily Bart, a beautiful *object*, a very expensive commodity; her death is equally pitiable and pitiful.

Amherst's own class consciousness, by contrast, is less elitist but also less secure. One sees this in the conflict he feels between his desire for socialist reform and his desire for Bessy. He denounces the "baneful paternalism" (194) necessary to capitalist modes of production but cannot admit to his own paternalistic domination of his wife. When it becomes clear that he cannot reform Bessy, that he cannot overpower her, one both sympathizes with him, since Bessy is marked as class antagonist, and questions his will-to-power, since he is shown as her male antagonist. While his class consciousness is clearly morally superior to that of Bessy, his gender consciousness is at times no less reactionary than hers.

His split consciousness is seen as even more problematic in his relationship with another woman, Justine Brent, like him someone born into the privileged class but who, because of circumstances and hard times, seems to "belong to none" (141). Amherst meets her before Bessy enters his life, when she is a nurse tending to a severely injured worker; and they immediately mirror each other's outrage over the treacherous relationship between classes. They then meet again a few years after his marriage to Bessy at a time when both feel alienated, Amherst because his politics have cost him his life of pleasure with Bessy, Justine because she also cannot realize a private life as well as her social agenda. Justine then becomes the mediator between Amherst and Bessy, a fitting role in that she too has split allegiances: she is radical sympathizer to Amherst's project, a fellow-traveller, but she is also Bessy's old schoolmate, an empathetic woman. Of the three, Justine alone comes slowly to understand the abysmal nature of the marriage: "That which was the essence of life to one was a meaningless shadow to the other; and the gulf between them was too wide for the imagination of either to bridge" (399). Like the other two, however, she wishes for simple escape from the battleground of opposing desires, but she is never as precipitant in her actions as they are, and so she remains with Bessy. Later, when Bessy is crippled after a fall from her horse Impulse, the name an obvious allusion to her own irresponsible and unthinking relation to husband and life, Justine must then reconsider her own relation to life and to death-in-life. In answer to Bessy's wish to die and believing Amherst would sanction her act, Justine kills Bessy with an overdose of morphia. In doing so, Justine revolts against the dictates of "society—science—religion" (418), all of which she feels to be extremely cruel forms of baneful paternalism. Justine's is, of course, the most radical and selfless act in the novel. She both frees Bessy from what she sees as soulless agony and as a consequence empowers Amherst who now inherits primary control of the mills.

Justine's act does not, however, resolve the conflicts first introduced in the novel; neither does her subsequent marriage to Amherst, even though it is a seemingly perfect wedding of ideologies. Justine, as the reader knows, has too much heart. Unlike Amherst, she responds to individual suffering, not only suffering in the abstract, and she acts accordingly and believes her acts to be for the good. In contrast, it is Amherst, not Justine, who suffers guilt over Bessy's death; it is Amherst who atones for his ill treatment of Bessy by making the mills her monument and who never realizes the utter inadequacy of that abstraction. Despite these crucial differences, they live together contentedly until the ghost of Bessy appears in the form of Stephen Wyant, the doctor in attendance at her death.

At this point, the plot twists become excruciatingly melodramatic. Wyant blackmails Justine because he has suffered a breakdown, made a worthless marriage, and lost all hope of attaining a respectable position. Further, he is addicted to drugs, an affliction he blames on her since she had earlier on both denied him her hand in marriage and his chance at "a big success" (502), Bessy's cure. Justine pays him off for a year, not because she considers her act wrong but because she cannot find a way to speak of her dilemma to Amherst, her inability to communicate intimating that their marriage is not as perfect as originally imagined. Finally, when Amherst learns from her that she gave Bessy an overdose, that she killed the wife he has recreated as the angel in his house, he can intellectually apprehend the motive for her action but cannot emotionally accept the consequences. Justine then realizes too late what an extremely conventional man he is, despite his advocacy of social reform and, not incidentally, euthanasia. As Elizabeth Ammons argues, "he epitomizes the deep resistance to the idea of equality that [Wharton] saw among even the most progressive American men. He plays at change, in both the industrial and the domestic worlds, but in the end prefers a world unchanged" (54).

Justine then, like Wharton's other martyr-women, effaces herself completely for his sake, first leaving him so that he might
complete the work which constitutes his sole sense of self and
then returning to him when he authorizes such a reunion. Theirs
is at the end not a radically new way of living but a life "of pitiful
compromises with fate, of concessions to old traditions, old beliefs, old charities and frailties" (624). Like Kate Orme of *Sanctuary*, they might be able to drain the marshes and thus preserve
the social health, but they act as conservators rather than as
reformers. For them the fruit of the tree of life is bittersweet,
and, as Ammons forcefully argues, for Justine "the fruit of the
tree of marriage is bitter, indeed" (55).

Ethan Frome (1911) is a visionary tale of unconventional love
which, similar to Lily Bart's story, details moral, emotional, and
actual poverty. It also asks the same questions as does *The Fruit
of the Tree*: "was there then no hope of lifting one's individual
life to a clearer height of conduct? Must one be content to think
for the race, and to feel only—feel blindly and incoherently—
for one's self?" (*Fruit* 526). It then offers a particularly despairing
answer to these questions.

Ethan Frome takes place in Starkfield, an obviously weighted
name, and the even more isolated farm of Frome. Life in Starkfield is described by the narrator as social negation in which, as
in Old New York, the appearance of collectivity disguises actual
individual alienation: "All the dwellers in Starkfield, as in more
notable communities, had had troubles enough of their own to
make them comparatively indifferent to those of their neigh-
bours" (11). Frome had, early in life, compromised himself to
fulfill social expectations, giving up a possible career outside of
Starkfield in order to support his physically and mentally ailing
parents. After their deaths and instead of escaping, he married
his cousin Zenobia, who quickly became yet another burden, and
then seemed to resign himself to spending the rest of his days
eking out a meager existence on a land far removed from modern life. Mattie Silver enters his world as servant to Zeena, and
Mattie, symbolically representative of light and life, acts as a
catalyst for his revolt against the strictures imposed on him by
his social group.

Early on in his affair, Frome believes his desired self, lover of

Mattie, can compatibly exist alongside his social self, husband of
Zeena, citizen of Starkfield. Like Lily Bart, Frome sees revolutionary ideals, embodied in Mattie as Selden did for Lily, as a
means of transcending his existence but also, as seen in Frome's
thoughts on his family's graveyard, a means of rationalizing morbidity and social imprisonment:

> "We never got away—how should you?" seemed to be written on every
> headstone; and whenever he went in or out of his gate he thought with
> a shiver: "I shall just go on living here till I join them." But now all
> desire for change had vanished, and the sight of the little enclosure
> gave him a warm sense of continuance and stability. (50)

However, Frome does not comprehend the innate power of the
collective over him (again, the clashing consciousnesses of the
private and public selves) or society's necessary maintenance,
however feeble that might be, of its traditional code of ethics for
the purpose of its own self-perpetuation. While Zeena is far from
being a beautiful object, she is still Frome's wife and therefore
the socially sanctioned object of his physical and monetary attention. In the eyes of Starkfield society, it is Mattie who is ex-
pendable, and thus so is Ethan's self-will and desire; this attitude
remains constant throughout and deceptively sympathetic in its
expression, or, as Mrs. Hale says, " 'if [Mattie had] died, Ethan
might ha' lived' " (181).

When Ethan is forced to choose between realization of his
individuality and obeisance to the collective will, he echoes Lily
Bart's inability to perceive her fate as anything other than predetermined: "The inexorable facts closed in on him like prison-
warders handcuffing a convict. There was no way out—none.
He was a prisoner for life" (134). His one decision, that of following Mattie's plan of freedom gained through suicide, is as
idealistically naive as Lily's initial response to Selden's republic
of the spirit. As is seen in the conclusion of both novels, the total
negation of self-responsibility coupled with limited social consciousness leads only to the false freedom of self-annihilation,
which, in turn, is an ineffectual revolt against the collective will.
Ethan's "epilogue in hell" (151), as Marius Bewley calls it, is not
moral retribution for immoral acts but only a Beckettian hellish

half-light existence reflecting Ethan's life from the outset of the tale and resulting from compromise of the awakened individual to his limited social consciousness. Wharton thus implicitly calls for the missing factor which would preclude such nihilistic tragedy: a reintegration of the awakened individual with the collective, an analysis of individual and collective experience, a new collective world view.

Summer (1917), privately known to Wharton and her friends as "the Hot Ethan" (*Letters* 385), pushes the oppositions seen in Wharton's early works one step further and offers a tentative, if ambiguous, solution to alienation and social disintegration. Again, *Summer* is a story of unconventional love, this time consummated, but in this case, it is also a love ultimately accepted by and assimilated into a mildly reintegrated society. The importance of *Summer* in the development of Wharton's analysis of society, reflected both in her style and content, lies in the fact that herein Wharton focuses on a complete social outcast: Charity Royall. There are no cushioning mediations between society and the individual as were present between Lily or Frome and their worlds. We are instead presented with an individual openly born into and brought up in states of alienation. Thus, *Summer* is necessarily Wharton's strongest statement up to this point concerning the realization of individuality and the search of the individual for security in a positive community.

Charity is the child of a convicted murderer and a "half human" (73) woman from the Mountain, a kind of actualized, corrupted republic of the spirit notable for its lawlessness, poverty, amorality, and social irresponsibility. As an act of charity, she was brought down from the Mountain and brought up by the Royalls in North Dormer, "an empty place" (9). As a young girl she almost escaped North Dormer by moving to a boarding school in Starkfield—an indication that *Summer*'s world is twice removed from modern life—but instead stayed with lawyer Royall after the death of his wife. Charity and Royall have a relationship analogous to that of Ethan and Zenobia, though one that is neither physically consummated despite Royall's attempts nor legally binding. Unlike Ethan, however, Charity, aware as Frome was of a larger world beyond her immediate confines, makes concerted and realistic efforts to finance her escape.

At the opening of the novel, Charity is in control of her world, the Royall household, though not a willing part of it. Her mental and moral self-reliance, as well as near financial independence, is compromised through an affair she has with Lucius Harney, a New Yorker who finally abandons her for his fiancée, and her consequent pregnancy. Charity first attempts to set up an abortion, but as this would be a negation of her love and life, she cannot go through with it. She then, in her search for a secure community in which to raise her child, returns to the Mountain, ostensibly her real home, but discovers it to be a perverse world of complete human alienation. Finally, she is again brought down from the Mountain by Royall, marries him, and returns to life in North Dormer with "a sense of peace and security" (273). At this point she seemingly carries within herself the dual consciousnesses of realized individual and secure member of society. However, while the ending appears to be the best of both worlds for Charity, a close reading exposes it to be, once again, a compromise of the individual resulting from unassimilable consciousnesses.

Before her affair with Lucius, Charity's sense of identity is based on an idealization of her own outcast status and her social independence. Her personal refuge lies precisely in her sense of self-worthlessness: she believes she has little to offer society, and she knows that society, so far, has given her nothing. She also feels no sense of responsibility toward others and has only a dim notion of what it means to be a rebel. Such limited perceptions of selfhood and social security help her maintain her naive dream of possible escape leading to a miraculously transformed life in the face of her actual penury and realistic social expectations. The experience with Lucius shatters her solipsistic and negative sense of self-identity; after their first meeting, her sense of selfhood shifts radically in that it is now predicated upon her sense of self as woman made for man, "what she was worth" to him (62). Thus, Charity replaces a negative asocial consciousness with that of the nineteenth-century ideological one of woman as mirror to man's desire: "she could imagine no reason for doing or not doing anything except the fact that Harney wished or did not wish it. All her tossing contradictory impulses were merged in a fatalistic acceptance of his will" (175). Their summer of passion in a deserted house seems to be Selden's republic lived out; however, it too proves to be "some bottomless abyss" (211) of asociality. Charity sees late in the affair that she has been a partner to only one facet of Lucius' life, his sexuality, and that in her role as lover and reflector of passion, she is alienated from the social Lucius and his world: "Behind the frail screen of her lover's caresses was the whole inscrutable mystery of his life: his relations with other people—with other women— his opinions, his prejudices, his principles, the net of influences and interests and ambitions in which every man's life is entan- gled" (197). She understands then the limitations of her new social consciousness, social in that she relates to another even if only as "other," but, in accord with ideological strictures, she sacrifices her lover for his sake. While her escape to the Mountain appears to be a revolt against this limited social consciousness, it is this same new collective identification which thwarts her reunion with the alienated beings there. Finally, her marriage to Royall is a reintegration of her social self within his collective, but this is effected at the cost of her admittedly naive ideals and her real self, in part awakened through her particular sensual experience, recalling Chopin's rebel women. As Margaret B. McDowell writes, "Charity's love affair has thus cost her her independence as a human being. She has, in effect, spent her life in one summer" (71).

Charity's final sacrifice of self to collective, her reestablishment in society for the sake of future generations, is possibly a positive one, but Wharton's ending does not speak clearly to this effect. Wharton suggests, however, that through individual kindness— that of Royall, for example—the social rebel might find a haven in which one could nurture the aftereffects or memory of per- sonal revolt—in this case, Charity and Royall raising Lucius' and Charity's child as their own. At the same time, that kindness is presented as highly suspect, as are many acts of charity. As John W. Crowley notes, "Royall's assumption that women are a form of property underlies all his actions regarding Charity, but he is never conscious of this assumption" (89). It is also impossible to overlook the incestuous impulse dramatized in Royall's pursuit of Charity, an impulse that is strangely effaced at the end when he offers Charity money and marriage. In short, the vicissitudes of her fate allow his purchasing of her as his child bride with child. As Crowley suggests, "Charity's recrossing the threshold of Royall's house . . . marks the death of her summer daydreams in the autumn moonlight"; "as Royall's wife, Charity has even less freedom than as his ward. All she does have is the material compensation that North Dormer men pay to women for their subjection" (95). In fact, as Wharton herself felt, the novel is less Charity's than Royall's (*Letters* 398): his subject position is continuously reconstituted whereas Charity remains always the object of desire within the story. It is clear, in any case, that society as yet has no understanding of woman's desire, that the sociosexual dichotomies are still effective, that scandal and revolt are recognized only by collective cooptation and then only after the fact.

The Reef (1912) brings Wharton's exploration of unconventional love to New York society, here transported to France and further isolated in one tomblike chateau. The locale is as important thematically as was Charity's social status; both are symbolic indications that Wharton is here dealing with stagnant or corrupted societies the members of which do not desire or effect change. This time Wharton offers implicit social criticism through her portrayal of individual relationships predicated again upon the ideological double standard and doubts concerning bourgeois or hegemonic morality.

The novel is also Wharton's most determinedly Jamesian or psychological work, so much so that Wharton wrote to a friend, "it's not *me*, though I thought it was when I was writing it" (*Letters* 284). The plot is not action but dissection, here of the consciousnesses of two characters: George Darrow and Anna Leath. Both had grown up in the same New York circle and had loved one another. However, Anna, in a naive swipe at social expectations, married Fraser Leath; he had appeared to be a social rebel totally unlike the too genteel Darrow. Her marriage proves to be loveless and conventional in its unconventionality. Leath, like Selden, advocated social revolt only because he was firmly and willfully entrenched in society and because such an attitude is an alluring pose. Leath then died, leaving Anna with a young daughter, an adult stepson, and a bone-chilling chateau. At the outset of the novel, George has been summoned to the Leath chateau; their first love is now to be consummated in marriage. However, George, put off without reason by Anna, has an affair with Sophie Viner. Months later George proposes to Anna who accepts, but their marriage plans are shattered when Anna discovers George's affair with Sophie, who is now governess to her child. The novel's set piece is the psychological portrayal of George and Anna at this climactic point of moral conflict.

Wharton constructs George's character as an emphatic embodiment of the patriarchal world view. He perceives women as falling into two categories, lady and whore, each having a straightforward value "to the more complex masculine nature" (25). George, at the time of his first planned reunion with Anna, has wearied of his genteel roué role. He sees his future marriage to Anna as a means of establishing himself anew in the social collective and continuity: "He was a little tired of experimenting on life; he wanted to 'take a line,' to follow things up, to centralize and concentrate, and produce results" (127). After he is rejected by Anna, he rationalizes his businesslike affair with Sophie as a necessary reaction against Anna's life-negating womanhood:

What were all her reticences and evasions but the result of the deadening process of forming a "lady"? The freshness he had marvelled at was like the unnatural whiteness of flowers forced in the dark. . . . She was still afraid of life, of its ruthlessness, its danger and mystery. She was still the petted little girl who cannot be left alone in the dark. . . . (28)

However, after his reconciliation with her, he sees these same repressive qualities as positive assets, primarily because she is now his property: "She was like a picture so hung that it can be seen only at a certain angle: an angle known to no one but its possessor. The thought flattered his sense of possessorship" (129). George, unlike Selden, privately admits to the fatuousness of his views, but he also revels in them. His attitudes and critical awareness of the same prove him to be in tune with his society. His arrogance, duplicity, and moral vacuousness are characteristics of those who are inherently irresponsible and unresponsive yet are acceptable to his society in which he is securely a charter member. He does not change throughout the novel, for there is no need that he should.

Wharton initially introduces Anna's character as a female counterpart to George's male chauvinism. Anna's life before Darrow had been one based solely on appearances consciously divorced from "the actual business of living" (94). However, despite her mentally sterile marriage to Leath, Anna is still partial to the illusions that love, that between husband and wife, "would one day release her from this spell of unreality" (86). Her nascent consciousness, then, is to be awakened through identification with a man and within a socially sanctioned relationship. After she accepts George's proposal, Anna's private emotional response resounds with true womanhood rhetoric:

She felt like testing him by the most fantastic exactions, and at the same moment she longed to humble herself before him, to make herself the shadow and echo of his mood. She wanted to linger with him in a world of fancy and yet to walk at his side in the world of fact. She wanted him to feel her power and yet to love her for her ignorance and humility. She felt like a slave, and a goddess, and a girl in her teens. . . . (124)

This is a potentially perfect genteel marriage, indeed, each member fulfilling ideologically-ordained roles, save for Sophie Viner, the one too real reminder of actuality.

Sophie destroys Anna's unconscious acceptance of the true womanhood world by offering an alternative to it. Her philosophy is that of pure individualism, in large part so because she is, like Mattie and Charity, outside of proper society. Her love for George, as she tells Anna, needs no moral justification or social valorization: " 'I wanted it—I chose it. He was good to me—no one was ever so good!' " (287) While Sophie is not, as some critics would have it, a "new woman"—she is too near a cipher for such a full-blooded concept—her radical consciousness is arguably superior to Anna's, an indication that Anna too is a personal cipher, a woman refiguring herself as stereotype. Sophie is both socially responsible—she does not use scandal against Anna's clan—and personally self-sufficient—she requires no partner in whom her identity is permanently subsumed. Anna's limited consciousness, on the other hand, calls for social duty only to her isolated society of three, perhaps destructively so, and personal dependence on George for her sense of identity.

Anna's confrontation with Sophie's self-realized, positive alternative world view or consciousness necessarily exposes her world—that of Leath and Darrow, her womanhood self and the like—as repressive, immoral, and alienating. Again, Wharton conjures up a vision of chaos and indeterminacy as Anna tries to reconcile her limited consciousness with a new and frighteningly open one: "She felt like a traveller on a giddy path between a cliff and a precipice: there was nothing but to go on" (339–340).

In the end, Wharton offers no resolution; the synthesis of clashing consciousnesses, a predominantly genteel one incorporating womanhood ideology assimilated within a modern, liberal world view, is seemingly impossible within the boundaries of this text. For all three characters, their experiences are, in different ways, tragedies culminating in isolation and desolation. The novel is remorseless, then, in its call for a new way of living, but it is also intensely pessimistic, so much so that the overwhelming futility the characters feel is transmitted too well to the reader. Wharton herself felt "sick about it—poor miserable lifeless lump that it is!" (*Letters* 284) and did not consider it an artistic success.

A brief look at one of Wharton's later short stories offers an important clarification of her attitude toward individual rebellion. In "The Long Run" (1916), Wharton shows the consequences of *not* revolting against social strictures and prescriptions: in the long run, one would come to despise "the rage of conformity" and to despair at having missed the actual business of living (II, 321). In each individual case, then, rebellion if it be done in search of selfhood is a potentially positive and necessary act. It is only inaction or complacency that leads to private tragedy. Furthermore, Wharton intimates in all these texts that what holds true for the individual does so as well for the collective. It is her world which is at fault if the end result of experience be incomprehensible despair or silence. If a society cannot assimilate the experiences of a Sophie Viner or Anna Leath or comprehend the self-desire of a Charity Royall or Ethan Frome, then it is as perverse a state of being as is Charity's Mountain or Selden's republic.

Wharton's *The Custom of the Country* (1913) studies Lily Bart's

world a decade later and the massive social transformations ef-
fectuated by the incursion and assimilation of new money society
into the old genteel one. This social analysis is implicitly presented in her account of Undine Spragg's meteoric rise from
Apex City through the New York 400 and the French Faubourg
Saint Germain to a commanding position in modern New York
society, from the dingy provinces to the dazzling center of urbane
life. Wharton continually counterposes several social milieus but
not, as one would expect, opposing world views. Again she focuses on the hegemonic ideology, the cult of true womanhood,
fundamental to all the social groups depicted. Wharton here
dissects a further manifestation of ideological types in her portrayal of Undine Spragg: the woman as social and financial entrepreneur, the beautiful object unmasked as rapacious
consumer. Like Sophie Viner who was an emotional entrepreneur, Undine is not the complete new woman despite her seemingly independent actions. Instead, she is a brilliant and
determined individual reacting against the moral limitations but
not the social advantages of patriarchal prescriptions.

Undine, as one character says, is "a monstrously perfect result
of the system: the completest proof of its triumph!" (208) She
is the all-American girl, her "pioneer blood" (56) complemented
by her "instinct of sex" (70), the consummate beautiful object
who realizes both the value and the self-aggrandizing use of her
social capital, a perfect personification of her society's materialism. However, despite Undine's highly developed sense of the
possible uses of capital, both social and economic, she is ignorant
of the forces of production behind it; like Lily Bart, she lacks
any sense of a real relation to life. Instead, and in accordance
with the custom of the country, Undine willfully divorces herself
from real business, that of Wall Street, and concerns herself
solely with social business, that of Fifth Avenue. Undine perceives this separation of appearance and reality as a positive given
as can be seen, for example, when she defines business: "*That*
was man's province; and what did men go 'down town' for but
to bring back the spoils to their women?" (44) It is clear, then,
that Undine's social consciousness reflects the genteel ideological
limitations concerning social realities and non-realities. It is only
her individual twist on ideology—"To have things had always

seemed to her the first essential of existence" (537)—that is, at times, at variance with the tradition of genteel appearances. She is motivated as well by the desire to have "what the others want" (100), which in all important instances necessitates taking away what others have. In this she is ruthless: "It was characteristic of her that she remembered her failures as keenly as her triumphs, and that the passionate desire to obliterate, to 'get even' with them, was always among the latent incentives of her conduct" (98). Undine as entrepreneur is too openly "the perfectly commercial item," as Cynthia Wolff writes, and the insatiable consumer (*Feast* 249). However, while she is the perfect product, she is by no means the exception to the rules. If Undine is only the ultimately perverse social citizen who desires assimilation into society because that world is the best buy on the market, then that society can be seen as inherently corrupt in its willingness to embrace her, to compromise its ethics for the sake of her money. The presentation of Undine's character is, in essence, Wharton's indictment of a world based on fluctuating values and relative morality, concepts which Undine capitalizes upon in her business, a world in which the only undisputed convention is not to sell oneself short. Society here is a killer's market.

Undine's business, of course, necessitates partnership with men. Her first marriage is an unmitigated disaster in terms of her making a socially and financially profitable match; she makes the unbelievable error of marrying for love, or what she takes to be love. Her father, an astute businessman, calculates the immediate gains for Undine, finds them nonexistent, and annuls the contract. Undine then moves to New York's Stentorian Hotel and, for a foothold in New York's 400, marries Ralph Marvell.

Marvell's gentility and love of romantic illusions are complemented with a sometimes perspicacious awareness of social actualities. He likens his class to "Aborigines" (73) clinging to limited and limiting rituals, incapable of revitalizing social conventions that would assure social survival. On the other hand, Marvell sees the new money class as "monstrous and factitious" (73) and as caught up in the game of appearances versus reality as is genteel New York. However, his social awareness translates in pragmatic terms only into an unmitigatedly pessimistic world view: "The daughters of his own race sold themselves to the Invaders; the daughters of the Invaders bought their husbands as they bought an opera-box. It ought all to have been transacted on the Stock Exchange" (78). Ralph is, therefore, twice divorced from the reality of life's business by virtue of his class standing and his negative consciousness. His attitude toward marriage to Undine is equally problematic in that his union is for him a fulfillment of patriarchal ideals and not, as the reader sees, a transcendence of self-alienation or an actualization of awakened consciousness:

he seemed to see her like a lovely rock-bound Andromeda, with the devouring monster Society careening up to make a mouthful of her; and himself whirling down on his winged horse—just Pegasus turned Rosinante for the nonce—to cut her bonds, snatch her up, and whirl her back into the blue.... (84)

He drastically miscalculates his role in Undine's redemption, figuring himself as the romanticized hero in a very old story rather than as Undine's ticket by which she gains admittance to a very new one.

Undine also marries naively, in her case for the satisfaction of her ideals of "amusement and respectability" (354). The difference between the two partners lies in their ability to comprehend the reality of their misalliance and to cut their losses. Ralph never fully surrenders his romantic view of Undine, but Undine pragmatically gives up Marvell, revealed to her after their marriage as having only the appearance of wealth and status, in order to negotiate her pursuit of the Big Deal.

Her next two paramours, while less idealistically romantic than Ralph, prove equally unsatisfying. Peter van Degen, an embodiment of the vulgar rich but socially secure class, seems a fair match for Undine's entrepreneurial self. The affair is also motivated for Undine by jealousy and a desire for revenge: van Degen's wife is Ralph's cousin, the woman, as is made all too clear, he should have married in that she is his social and ideological complement. Their affair is openly negotiated on "the installment plan," van Degen paying Undine's bills for future sexual favors, what van Degen alludes to as accumulated interest

(231). However, Undine is revealed as too ruthless a business-woman even for him. Undine chooses to pay off her interest while Ralph lies near death, for Undine a "bold move . . . as carefully calculated as the happiest Wall Street 'stroke' " (364). For van Degen, it is too pointedly an indication of his relative value to her and possible future treatment at her hands; her actions shatter his ideal of a morally, or immorally, compatible mate in that she proves to be much too unwomanly in her desire to be in on the kill. He leaves her, after he has collected his interest, of course.

Undine, aware of "her diminished trading capacity" (361) after the van Degen affair, then latches onto Marquis Raymond de Chelles and marries him. This act is a social and financial disaster equal to the Marvell escapade. De Chelles expects her to be the embodiment of the true woman, in this case not Ralph's victim awaiting rescue but the selfless mirror reflecting his superiority, and, as with Ralph, Undine discovers her new marriage offers none of the expected social benefits—Undine as mistress of a palatial hôtel in Paris and centerpiece of society—but only the limitations—Undine as isolated chatelaine in a chilly country chateau and mute wife to a faithless husband.

Undine's last marriage brings her full circle in that she reunites with her first husband, Elmer Moffatt, now the "billionaire Railroad King" (585). Wharton makes clear throughout the book that these two entrepreneurs are the only characters who truly understand and accept one another; they are seemingly equals in the worlds of social and financial business. However, even this marriage is not mutually satisfying. Moffatt, the "greatest American collector" (530), is content in having finally acquired "the best" (538): Undine. Yet, despite a new Parisian hôtel complete with de Chelles' ancestral tapestries and a Fifth Avenue mansion which is "an exact copy of the Pitti Palace, Florence" (586), Undine remains unconvinced that she has not sold herself short again: "She had everything she wanted, but she still felt, at times, that there were other things she might want if she knew about them. And there had been moments lately when she had had to confess to herself that Moffatt did not fit into the picture" (591).

By the conclusion, this speculation becomes reality, and the saga of Undine Spragg's search for self-realization through conscious objectification is left unresolved. This is only to be expected; as Wharton has postulated, Undine's world view is based on voracious materialism and a degenerate variation of nineteenth-century womanhood ideology. Undine's experiences prove dissatisfying and alienating precisely because her limited consciousness advocates, despite her own actions, rigid sexual roles: the woman as prize object possessed by (and of) the man who can afford and maintain her object position. She does not seek a subject position "in the very middle of the picture" yet is dismayed when she finds herself repeatedly merely "a parenthesis" on the margins (207). She also buys into the separation of appearance from reality, the social picture given precedence over self-delineation. Those who share Undine's world view, those who maintain her belief in the primal nature of this "custom of the country" (206), remain disunited since there are no clear social or moral horizons by which any one may obtain a foothold in reality. This alternative variant of limited social consciousness is, then, neither the answer to social stagnation nor to individual alienation: "under all the dazzle a tiny black cloud" remains (594).

Wharton's two short stories of social entrepreneurship support this view. "The Introducers" (1906) is mildly ironic but finally romantic fiction in which two social climbers who plan to marry each other's wealthy charge fall in love instead. It is noteworthy that in this tale both characters reject their materialistic lifestyles at the disclosure of their mutual affection. "Les Metteurs en Scène" (1908) is a darker retelling of the same plot. Here, the female entrepreneur, Blanche Lambart, eventually inherits a cool million from a new money girl Blanche introduced into society. However, the male entrepreneur, Jean Le Fanois, whom Blanche loves, must reject her offer of marriage and final social/financial security; he has already affianced himself to the rich girl's dowdy mother. Society is, as Marvell conjectured and Blanche learns, a killer's market in which the house always beats the player. In Wharton's world, monetary and social success is fleeting; more importantly, and even in these texts about ultimate social bounders, self-realization is impossible because the boundaries of social and self-fulfillment remain ever limited.

One sees this to be the case even with *The Glimpses of the Moon*, perhaps Wharton's strangest version of the entrepreneur tale in that it blends elements of the above stories and *The Custom of the Country* with the pathos of *The House of Mirth*. Begun in 1916 and published in 1922, *The Glimpses of the Moon* is the story of two young but poor socialites who contract a marriage meant to last one year for their "mutual advantage" (49)—for the pleasure of their licit companionship and the profit of public coupling, both in terms of immediate monetary gains and longterm social connections. Wharton, in a 1921 letter to Bernard Berenson, states that the novel "tries to picture the adventures of a young couple who believe themselves to be completely affranchis & up-to-date, but are continually tripped up by obsolete sensibilities, & discarded ideals.—A difficult subject, which of course seemed the easiest in the world when I began it" (*Letters* 446). Indeed, Wharton's attempt to animate characters both emancipated and "incorrigibly old-fashioned" (324) proves not particularly suc-cessful precisely because of its reliance on the same old moral contradictions and gender differences to move the action for-ward and its inability to dramatize those contradictions and dif-ferences beyond what she had already done so in texts prior to *The Custom of the Country*.

Susy Branch and Nick Lansing contract what she calls their "partnership" (49), in essence, to buy time for themselves: their marriage gifts will allow them a splendid year together, their heightened social profile will offer them opportunities to meet wealthier second spouses. Their experiment, as it is called throughout the novel, begins well enough, each partner seeming to understand the other intuitively: Nick feels "the sense, be-tween himself and her, of a kind of free-masonry of precocious tolerance and irony. They had both, in early youth, taken the measure of the world they happened to live in: they knew just what it was worth to them and for what reasons, and the com-munity of these reasons lent to their intimacy its last exquisite touch" (17). Their intimacy, however, is from the outset also constrained by what Nick sees as their "business contract" (317): they can have no future, such as Nick's quickly suppressed dream of " 'settling down to family cares' " (3); their immediate "moral freedom" and happiness is predicated upon a freedom from "material cares" (216), and that they do not possess. Even during their first few blissful weeks together, they are at the mercy of rich friends' largesse, and both, through Susy's actions, are tainted by the immorality of others. Most crucially, they make the mistake of falling in love; their marriage despite its initial coolly contractual nature becomes for them an "awakening" (193), a union highly suggestive of Selden's republic of the spirit. The contrary natures of their love and business relationships then prove self-destructive. As Nick comes to feel,

It had been the tragedy of their relation that loving her roused in him ideals she could never satisfy. He had fallen in love with her because she was, like himself, amused, unprejudiced and disenchanted; and he could not go on loving her unless she ceased to be all these things. From that circle there was no issue, and in it he desperately revolved (284).

Susy, in turn, experiences a birth of self in her love for Nick but it is a self tied to the true womanhood ideals which Nick clearly admires. Her flawed moral sensibility, then, proves unacceptable even though, as she points out to him, she acts only for his sake. Under stress of the contradictory demands facing her, "the queer edifice of Susy's standards tottered on its base—she honestly didn't know where fairness lay, as between so much that was foul" (38). To complicate matters further, and despite the fact that Nick admits that they are "born parasites, both" (111), he also believes in "the difference—the fundamental difference" between men and women. That difference, a peculiarly negative reading of true man- and womanhood, is that women do "people's dirty work for them...for favours in return" (108) and men do not. He leaves Susy once he learns of the moral compromises she has made to maintain their republic of the spirit, yet he is not appalled by his own participation in a marriage as "business contract" since that experiment was not his idea and his love for her was swift in coming and, he feels, sincere. In previous alliances he had felt at first "the hunter" and then "the prey" (65), and one sees that with Susy these positions are displaced by that of the wronged lover, the man done in by a woman's dirty work.

Though Wharton at first seems to focus on Nick's disillusionment and superior morality, his reflections also serve to shift attention to Susy and woman's lot. Nick comes to understand, as does the reader, that Susy's is a harder life than his, one of necessary compromises and dulled sensibilities, a life made harder precisely because she is a poor woman and thus dependent upon the "tribe," particularly its women, for her sustenance. She is also, like Lily Bart and Undine Spragg, a social product seemingly incapable of finding self-realization either outside her social circle or within herself alone. More to the point, she believes herself unequal to Nick despite their so-called "partnership": he is the only man who maintains himself "in the show and yet outside of it" (219), a human embodiment, as Selden was for Lily, of her vague ideals. Late in the novel, we learn that Susy's "disgusted recoil from the standards and ideals of everybody about her...had flung her into her mad marriage with Nick" (216). He, then, represents for her the Other, the republic of the spirit, her consciousness awakened by him and dependent on his nurturance. When he abandons her, she is not simply the wronged lover, suffering as he does the chills and fevered anguish of lost love. She becomes, at most, a trace of herself, translated into "Nick's Susy, and no one else's" (270), and, at worst, nothing, "from the other side of the grave...a ghost among ghosts" (271). She becomes, in short, another Lily Bart, wandering into abysses of solitude, trying "to get used to being dead: that seemed to be her immediate business" (281).

Unlike Lily, she does not die, although she does find a community in which she becomes "temporary mother" (296), an act recalling Lily's dream/death child, and she also renounces "money, luxury, fashion, pleasure:...the four cornerstones of her existence" (134), experiencing, in other words, social death. In fact, Nick and Susy reconcile at the end because marriage for them is "something—inexorable" (348), and in the bathetic penultimate scene, they virtually shout out that theirs is a true love which cannot be denied and that defies all previous experience. Each then gives up a wealthy lover and the secure future promised by a British count and another rich girl from Apex City, Cora Hicks. They seem to have refound their republic. Yet, Wharton's work again ends on a note of loss, limitation, irreconcilable difference.

The positive reconciliation is strangely qualified at the end by a last set of contradictions: Susy again morally compromises them in order to secure money for their reunion; Nick feels again the fundamental difference between men and women in their "two ways of loving" (364), as he perceives Susy's self-abnegation and feels remorse at losing Cora Hick's love and money. The last scene is of Susy and Nick in their room at Fontainebleau—a site of refound money, luxury, fashion, pleasure—momentarily free of the five children under Susy's care: "They leaned on the sill in the darkness, and through the clouds, from which a few drops were already falling, the moon, labouring upward, swam into a space of sky, cast her troubled glory on them, and was again hidden" (364). As the images suggest, theirs, evidently, is to be a fleeting happiness, its transient nature symbolized both in the moon imagery and the sham family with which they are burdened. Theirs is an already beclouded awakening of desire. Neither they nor their world has changed much, and their reunion seems a somewhat hopeless capitulation to moral compromise:

the fault was doubtless neither hers nor his, but that of the world they had grown up in, of their own moral contempt for it and physical dependence on it, of his half-talents and her half-principles, of the something in them both that was not stout enough to resist nor yet pliant enough to yield (166).

Nick will go back to writing *The Pageant of Alexander*, his manly tale, and being loved by Susy, while Susy, like other women in their society, will become more and more the "harmless vampire" (145), the woman who exists "just to love" (292) and to feed on those who create, however meagerly. The fundamental differences between true women and true men are maintained; the whole business of such differences has merely begun again.

This business is taken up in her next novel, arguably her greatest. The works discussed thus far, including those by Chopin, offered analyses of progressive stages of social consciousness within a time of social and economic transition. These variational consciousnesses—whether individual or collective, quiescent or awakened—were seen to be ultimately limited and alienating in that they reflected either estranging ideologies or moral inanition. None of these works presented explicitly an alternative consciousness radical enough to counteract alienation and to promote positive sexual and social reform. However, these works were literally stories and novels of social change, seen in both Chopin's and Wharton's content and analytical style; it is to be expected that realist writers would focus upon the social lacks and limits rather than on socialist or radical ideals. Wharton's *The Age of Innocence* (1920) continues to enlarge her social chronicle in that it presents Old New York in its heyday and a brief glimpse at the modern society of the late 1910s. This most famous of her works elaborates upon the social criticism presented in her earlier novels in that it offers both a realistic reevaluation of her own genteel culture and a tentatively optimistic view of a new American society and modern world. It is, as Wharton wrote to Bernard Berenson, "a 'simple & grave' story of two people trying to live up to something that was still 'felt in the blood' at that time" (*Letters* 433).

The *Age of Innocence* is also simply the story of a conventional man torn between his love for a social rebel and his relationship with his ideological mate. Wharton had previously utilized this love-triangle plot device in her historical epic, *The Valley of Decision* (1902), and in her social reform novel, *The Fruit of the Tree* (1907). In each case, unconventional love—Odo's for Fulvia, Amherst's for Bessy and Justine—was compromised by the man's inability to surrender fully his traditional world view. Similarly, in *The Age of Innocence*, Newland Archer can never fulfill his love for Ellen Olenska precisely because he cannot pull himself out of "the rage of conformity." In all three novels, compromise arises, for both men and women, because of their conscious acceptance but incomplete comprehension of hegemonic ideology and its power. *The Age of Innocence* offers a harsher social critique than do the other two texts, however, in that it sets up the ideology of separate spheres, the foundation of male supremacist ideology, only to explode it. Further, Wharton shows her readers that the price of conformity is as exacting for some men as it is for some women; in Newland Archer she offers the reader her most sympathetic male figure.

As Josephine Donovan writes, "the ironic title refers to a prelapsarian age; the novel is set in New York in the 1870s, but the

'innocence' of the title is seen by Wharton to be fraudulent..."
(75). Old New York is here portrayed as steeped in convention;
genteel customs are still supreme despite the dim but visible
Invaders on the social horizon. The ruling traditions appear to
be private and public honesty, bourgeois morals and taste, collective cohesion. In reality, genteel manners are a mask disguis-
ing hypocrisy, immorality, gross materialism, and collective
tyranny. It is again a society already advocating appearance over
reality: "stylishness was what New York most valued" (61). Further, it is a world in which actuality is manipulated in order to
save appearances: "In reality they all lived in a kind of hiero-
glyphic world where the real thing was never said or done or
even thought, but only represented by a set of arbitrary signs"
(45). Indeed, as one sees by the end, Newland's society is based
on the symbolic sacrifice of too real individuals, the "taking life
'without effusion of blood' " (335), if this be necessary for collective show and survival. The class motto of New York is succinctly put by Newland's mother: "if we don't all stand together,
there'll be no such thing as Society left" (51). This sacrificing of
individuals to the tribal needs occurs most prominently at Ellen's
casting-out dinner, but one also sees it in the maneuvering of
Newland into a position of complicity, a sacrifice of himself in
which he unconsciously assists.

Newland Archer, at the outset, is a socially secure "dilettante"
(4) and as fatuous a male ideologue as are Lawrence Selden and
George Darrow. He is engaged to May Welland who is, for her
time, a perfect "product of the system" (8). Newland's attitude
toward her is equally perfect in its ideological purity; he sees
her as his future possession ideally constructed of "abysmal purity" (7), "whiteness, radiance, goodness" (24), "truth...reality
...the life that belonged to him" (141), "peace, stability, com-
radeship and the steadying sense of an unescapable duty" (207).
This, of course, before the Fall: after meeting Ellen Olenska, a
social outcast of good family lineage, these positive values become for Newland negative and sterile.

Newland does not then come to despise May herself, since he
is incapable of seeing her individual self, but only the collective
conspiracy which she embodies for him, that conspiracy necessarily born out of the genteel ideology exacting specific sexual/

social roles for all individuals within separate spheres. Newland first faults May for being part of a matriarchal plot against male self-will:

And he felt himself oppressed by this creature of factitious purity, so cunningly manufactured by a conspiracy of mothers and aunts and grandmothers and long-dead ancestresses, because it was supposed to be what he wanted, what he had a right to, in order that he might exercise his lordly pleasure in smashing it like an image made of snow. (46)

Newland sees male power, in other words, as merely a female gift to men; his self-image is thus tainted by association with female will. Newland, of course, denies any personal complicity in this state of affairs, and even though he sometimes spouts liberation rhetoric, his sympathies at this point lie only with himself and the male world as he does battle with what he perceives as the repulsively feminine world embodied in May:

It would presently be his task to take the bandage from this young woman's eyes, and bid her look forth on the world. But how many generations of the women who had gone to her making had descended bandaged to the family vault? He shivered a little, remembering some of the new ideas in his scientific books, and the much-cited instance of the Kentucky cave-fish, which had ceased to develop eyes because they had no use for them. What if when he had bidden May Welland to open hers, they could only look out blankly at blankness? (83)

Newland both damns and supports, then, the ideology of separate spheres for women and men, an especially false construct in his case since both worlds are clearly inscribed within the same circle. Indeed, as is quickly made clear, Newland is less afraid of May's emptiness than of his own two-dimensional "character" which his relationship with her brings to light. Newland is repulsed by May because she reflects his own blindness and his particular "truth" and "reality," "the life that belonged to him" (141). In short, he is terrorized by the realization that their supposedly separate worlds are one in which there is seemingly no space for individual desire or vision. In answer to her praise of his individualist stance, Newland exposes what it is in May and

in himself which is irremediable: " 'Original! We're all as like
each other as those dolls cut out of the same folded paper. We're
like patterns stencilled on a wall' " (83).

Newland is correct, however, in sensing a conspiracy against
himself, but he is deluded in thinking women the sole perpe-
trators simply because they are the most visible actors in the plot
to keep him within and useful to his society. He is himself an
actor within that conspiracy, realizing too late his function in
maintaining the society in which he is privileged enough to exist.
As he comes to see, "In the rotation of crops there was a recognized season for wild oats; but they were not to be sown more
than once" (305) and that one time is to be in service to the
reapers: his individual desire, his will to desire, must be subor-
dinated to the tribal will to survive. His utter inability to affect
that society in any way other than to surrender his seed for its
"crops," his utter inability to effect self-realization, blinded as he
has been and continues to be by his own limited consciousness,
turns him both against and to woman, "the subject creature . . .
versed in the arts of the enslaved" (305). Only with women can
Newland act out the fantasies of his subjugation or of his mastery.

In a perversely irresponsible act, Newland marries May, this
despite his belief that their union is predicated on "a dull association of material and social interests held together by ignorance on the one side and hypocrisy on the other" (44–45). Since
he believes that May has been made for him but not by him, she
is made to serve him both as his oppressor and as the scapegoat
of his disillusionment. It comes as no surprise that Newland
experiences his marriage as "the same black abyss yawned before
him, and he felt himself sinking into it, deeper" (186). His complicity through his marriage with the hegemony makes of his
life an "endless emptiness" (227). Newland, however, does not
realize this fully until the end of his life; he only intuits in his
youth that his way of being has made of him a walking corpse.
As he tells May early on in their marriage: " 'I *am* dead—I've
been dead for months and months' " (295).

On the other hand, Ellen provokes his social self and finally
revitalizes his individual self, if only for a short time. At first he
responds to her as would any other genteel, chivalrous man. He

is drawn into association with her by his relationship with May and at the outset of their friendship, counsels Ellen to fit herself, as he has done, to society or to be outcast again: " 'one can't make over society.... The individual, in such cases, is nearly always sacrificed to what is supposed to be the collective interest; people cling to any convention that keeps the family together' " (112). Newland is not then totally aware of how firmly set he is within the larger family, society; neither is he conscious of the structures of power surrounding Ellen, those which she fully comprehends. With her, he does not come to understand the true separation of female and male worlds—that predicated upon desire—or her attempt to coexist peacefully on the edges of both spheres. Instead, he attempts to remake her in his image rather than finding himself through their relationship. For instance, he soon figures her simply as a helpless female who needs a knight such as he: "she stood before him as an exposed and pitiful figure, to be saved at all costs from farther wounding herself in her mad plunges against fate" (96). That she is an orphan and an outcast fits beautifully into his fantasy. And so he places her on the pedestal of his affections, the one from which he has dethroned May. He then begins to play out the role of romantic lover, supposedly ceding to her his power and will, that which May stole from him, while in actuality he does battle against her defenses against him.

For example, in their first major love scene, Newland is spurned and then envisions himself as most despairing and desperate lovers do, as on the edge of nothingness: "He felt as though he had been struggling for hours up the face of a steep precipice, and now, just as he had fought his way to the top, his hold had given way and he was pitching down headlong into darkness" (174). Even though Ellen has tried to teach him "the need of thinking himself into conditions incredibly different from any that he knew" (104), Newland cannot even with her accept responsibility for his own acts or see beyond his romantic delusions and his limited consciousness. In a later assault on her sense of self and responsibility, and in a curious inversion of his criticism of May, he faults Ellen for destroying his secure world while denying him hers. He tells her, " 'You gave me my first

glimpse of a real life, and at the same moment you asked me to
go on with a sham one. It's beyond human enduring—that's all' "
(242).

In essence, Ellen awakens his dormant sense of selfhood
achievable within an alternative reality beyond the confines of
New York. Indeed, in her home, dress, manners, presentation
of self—again, all matters of appearance—she comes to embody
for him potential self-fulfillment through "the actual business of
living":

for the first time Archer found himself face to face with the dread
argument of the individual case. Ellen Olenska was like no other woman,
he was like no other man: their situation, therefore, resembled no one
else's, and they were answerable to no tribunal but that of their own
judgment. (306)

However, since he is incapable of matching action to realization,
he then constructs a new fantasy, one as self-serving as the previous versions. After his marriage, Ellen is enshrined in Newland's particular republic of the spirit: "he had built up within
himself a kind of sanctuary in which she throned among his
secret thoughts and longings" (262). It is clear by the end that
Newland has not loved Ellen Olenska for her individuality but
merely as another objectified ideal, for he can never truly comprehend that which is "like nothing that he was accustomed to
look at (and therefore able to see)" (71). Newland, in short,
remains self-deceived on all accounts, and his inability to relinquish repressive idealism and romanticism for pragmatic action
is made evident to the resisting reader through Wharton's
straightforward yet complex presentation of Newland's two
women. Their realities and experience first complement and
then counteract Newland's oppressive world view.

Ellen, while admittedly in love with Newland, seeks only social
security and not another chance at social revolt. She understands
that the world of women, seen for example in the sphere of
Catherine Mingott, is still necessarily aligned with the world of
men so that it might survive. She is not, however, a totally passive
object: she strives throughout the story to maintain her personal
sense of integrity and self while simultaneously making over

society in small ways so that she can in turn find a comfortable
position in that world. To this effect, she is perfectly willing to
sacrifice her desire: as she tells Newland, " 'I can't love you unless
I give you up' " (173), a statement of foresight and not evasion
as was Robert Lebrun's to Edna Pontellier. She does so first by
continuously reminding him of his reality, May and his position
in society, and ultimately by abdicating her personal love and
social security, returning to an outcast's life. Ellen both understands self-desire and responsibility to self and others whereas
Newland only feels desire and a longing for self. She counters
Newland's idealism with pragmatism and logic—" 'we'll look, not
at visions, but at realities' " (289)—and in responding to his romantic view of an illicit affair, finally lays the illusive and ill-used
republic of the spirit to rest:

[Newland says,] "I want—I want somehow to get away with you into a
world where words like that—categories like that—won't exist. Where
we shall be simply two human beings who love each other, who are the
whole of life to each other; and nothing else on earth will matter." She
drew a deep sigh that ended in another laugh. "Oh, my dear—where
is that country?" (290)

Ellen knows that such utopian or romantic dreams are socially
futile since they cannot be actualized. She has been "beyond"
(291) Newland's world, and she realizes that one must live within
one's society or be alienated, observe the amenities even if they
be inanities or be without a *modus vivendi*. One must do so, that
is, while one must also seek to transform one's society, albeit if
only in small ways. Ellen's tragedy, though she would not call it
that, results from her singularity: except for the aged and the
eccentric, she has no community in which to position herself, no
community with which she might effect social change. She remains throughout an orphan in search of family.

Similarly, May is motivated by a desire for community, and
she is clearly not the helpless innocent Newland believes her to
be; neither is she at all passive in her fulfillment of ideological
prescription. Only at Ellen's casting-out farewell dinner given
by May does Newland realize that May has understood him all
along and that she has actively but not maliciously conspired

against Ellen and him in order to protect her immediate and extended family, society. So too does Newland learn after May's death that she had comprehended his affections for both her and Ellen and that she, like Ellen, had done only what she believed to be right. Newland as well after the departure of Ellen does the right thing: he returns to the woman made for him, May, and fulfills the roles assigned him. He becomes Newland Archer, the good husband, father, social citizen. They all force themselves to live good lives. Each woman, as well as Newland, fulfills ideological roles: martyr, moral superior, beloved object, the ideal. They are all complicit, then, in maintaining the hegemonic world view, and each suffers accordingly. However, Ellen also comprehended and opposed strict ideological adherence, at the same time refusing to fall victim to the alienating experience of blind, unreflective passion. Instead, what was first shown to the reader as her self-eccentricity is in the end revealed as a hopeful self-realization effected by a willful woman secure in a new land. There she seems to have found a community, though it is one which remains invisible, not yet inscribable.

It is at the end, a generation later and after the Lily Barts and Undine Spraggs, that Newland assimilates and evaluates his life experiences. After Ellen, Newland had lived a good life with May and unlike the majority of Wharton's characters had worked toward social reform. His genteel world gives way to the new money society and the world of new women. His final philosophical reading of social evolution is that "there was good in the old ways" (347) but "good in the new order too" (349). More important, however, is his realization that strict fulfillment of social duties had only served to establish him firmly in "a deep rut" (351), the anonymity of conformity. His unthinking complicity with patriarchal ideology costs Newland self-fulfillment, resulting in "an inarticulate lifetime" (356), Wharton's most pointed warning to men of the penalties of power. Newland comes to understand this not only through May but for himself: "Something he knew he had missed: the flower of life" (347). Yet his struggle with consciousness, as well as that of May and Ellen, is not without fruition. In the nurturing of a less repressive and more dynamic social order—in Newland's own work and in his son Dallas' upbringing—there is the potential realization of a humanistic, socially responsive consciousness denied Newland in his own life, a consciousness that would obliterate individual self-effacement and effect the full articulation of both male and female experience.

Wharton does not offer Newland absolution for his complicity; she does, however, show that life is a continuum, a dynamic web of action and reaction, potentially a revolutionary process of transcendence. Even though Newland cannot climb up to Ellen's level at the end, Wharton gives the reader a glimpse of a new structure of feeling, a positive world in which woman's will and desire are central and no longer marginal, in which both men and women can indeed dare and defy and yet live. Thus does Wharton, by calling into question both the conventional and the transgressive, struggle with her form—her particular set of arbitrary signs—and content—the full inscription of human relations. In this her pivotal work, she, like Chopin, subtly traversed literary and ideological boundaries, revealed in sharp detail what she knew of the human condition, and called yet again for quiet revolution. *The Age of Innocence* does not celebrate some mythic prelapsarian way of being, does not invest all value in a looking backward. Instead, it raises very important questions about how one might live not only a good but a full life in a postlapsarian world.

In her post–1920 work, Wharton continued searching for means of transcendence, exploring two further possible avenues which might offer security and self-fulfillment. As many critics have pointed out, several of these late novels do little more than recapitulate themes seen in earlier works. *The Glimpses of the Moon* has already been discussed as a flawed rewriting of *The House of Mirth* and *The Custom of the Country*. As Elizabeth Ammons also notes, *The Mother's Recompense*, published in 1925, is "in many ways a reworking and synthesis of *The Reef* and *The Age of Innocence*" (158). While Wharton might appear to be trapped in old materials, one element is strikingly new—her focus on the maternal sphere. It is not an unwarranted shift in perspective, however. In the pre–1920 works, Wharton analyzed almost in full the set of relations obtaining between women and men. These remained for her self-limiting and, in some cases, self-negating. It should not be surprising, then, that she turned full

attention to the one fundamentally different role of woman—
that of mother—already suggested in abortive scenes in the earlier works. After all, in the true womanhood world, becoming a
mother was equivalent to finding true self and pure, total love.

One sees this, for instance, in Lily's dream of a child and a
community: to be a mother is not to be alone, without purpose
or desire. One also recalls, on the other hand, the many negative
or compromised mothers of the early texts. The preeminent
example would be Undine who at first rejects pregnancy and
maternity as an intensely unwanted interruption of her narcissistic pursuit of self-aggrandizement and who then later uses her
son in order to effect her third marriage. Her son's sense of loss
at the end as he searches for his mother in newspaper reports
is profound and occasions deep sympathy from the reader,
moreso than that one feels for his father who should not have
been, by virtue of his age, the innocent his son must be. The
reader naturally takes the side of the child against the bad
mother. What is most disturbing in the case of this negative
mother, however, is that Undine has been described to the reader
as the "perfect product of the system." Luckily, for the sake of
the system's children, she also appears to be singular in that she
is *the* perfect product. A less atypical mother might be May in
The Age of Innocence, whose fortuitous pregnancy arrests Newland's flight from her. She is presented at the end as the good
mother, one who dutifully preserved the family, the cornerstone
of the system, and raised her children well even though in doing
so she compromised herself and her husband. They live out
successfully the American Dream, but it is one, for the parents,
that is qualified by loss: May dies, and Newland admits of himself
that he has missed the "flower of life." Still, as the novel's conclusion suggests, theirs are less damaged lives than those of Paul
Marvell de Chelles Moffatt or his mother, lives that have made
a positive difference unlike that of Lily Bart. May's maternity
and Newland's consequent entrapment as father is, then, a more
sympathetic reading of the old family romance. Motherhood,
nonetheless, is not presented in a particularly glorified fashion.

The post–1920 works explore much further the position of
mother and the dilemma of maternity. Again, it is not surprising
that Wharton's characterizations continue to be intensely critical

and realistic rather than sentimentalized cant. Though never a
mother herself, Wharton seems all too aware of the contradictory
desires which constitute that sacred figure. For example, in *The
Glimpses of the Moon*, Susy regains, she believes, a sense of self
and control when she enters the community of children. Acting
as governess to the Fulmer children is also her equivalent of
penance for her sins with and against Nick: she loses herself in
her role as "temporary mother" (296), which exacts from her
constant attention to the mundane, continual needs of children.
However, despite her position of authority and maturity, one
sees that motherhood is for her perhaps self-advancement but
also regression: " 'mothering' on a large scale would never, she
perceived, be her job. Rather it gave her, in odd ways, the sense
of being herself mothered, of taking her first steps in the life of
immaterial values which had begun to seem so much more sub-
stantial than any she had known" (298). As has already been
argued, the regressive side of her reinvented self comes to the
foreground in the conclusion which reinstates the old material
and sensual values, the "temporary" children abruptly shoved
into the background once they have served their purpose of
maternalizing Susy in Nick's eyes: "a thing apart, an uncondi-
tioned vision, the eternal image of the woman and the child"
(319).

Is the reader to assume, then, as Elizabeth Ammons does, that
Wharton believes "women are meant to be mothers" and that
she promotes this belief in the late novels (162)? Surely, the
compromised happy-ever-after ending of *The Glimpses of the
Moon* argues against this generalization; so does her characterization of mothers in *The Old Maid (The 'Fifties)* (1924), a novella
in which the birth mother painfully cedes her position to the
adoptive mother for the sake of her daughter's happiness and
at the cost of her own. Even the adoptive mother is less self-
realized through her children than she is through the memory
of a socially unacceptable man's love for her. As Delia thinks to
herself, "And then the babies; the babies who were supposed to
'make up for everything,' and didn't—though they were such
darlings, and one had no definite notion as to what it was that
one had missed, and that they were to make up for" (82). Maternity does not, for Wharton, magically erase loss. *The Mother's*

Recompense (1925) stands as further evidence against Ammon's interpretation. It details another rebirth of self through motherhood but is much less ambiguous in its reading of the regressive self-loss required of mothers, what Wharton at one point calls "the blessed anonymity of motherhood" (81). It also goes far beyond being a simple study of a parent's confusing relationship with the child, such as is presented in *A Son at the Front* (1923). Instead, Wharton focuses on the complex desires which constitute motherhood in conflict with the even more complex desires which delimit individuation, a conflict which, for Wharton, seems inevitably to lead to renunciation of all desire, a willful hurling of one's self into the abyss of solitude. One need, of course, only recall Newland's last scene of estrangement to understand that Wharton is in this new novel carrying an old theme further.

The novel opens on Kate Clephane, a middle-aged woman, in "her shabby cramped room in the third-rate Hôtel de Minorque et de l'Univers" (3), arising to yet another day's work of circumventing "the humdrum, the prosaic and the dreary" (5). Having deserted her husband and daughter eighteen years before, she is a self-exile who still considers herself "the 'good sort' " of woman (4) and whose universe is a life "chiefly with women of her own kind" (4). She considers herself somewhat superior to her situation and community in that she maintains "her pride" (4), even though her life as 'other,' as self-willed outcast, has been marked by "all the scheming, planning, ignoring, enduring, accepting, which had led her in the end to—this" (6). "This" is her essentially empty life, superficially filled with social engagements which offer her "escape from reality and durability" (5). Besides the affair which occasioned her flight from family and one other attachment, she has led a blameless life. That one other affair, however, was her greatest moment, surpassing in intensity of passion her marriage and maternity: "For the first time, when she met him, her soul's lungs seemed full of air. . . . At thirty-nine her real self had been born; without him she would never have had a self" (18). She maintains that sense of self in the face of his desertion; indeed, her sense of self as lover-beloved is the only source of meaning in her life—until the incident which initiates the novel's action occurs. Kate is abruptly recalled to the old world by a cable from her daughter. Following the death of her husband and the old Mrs. Clephane, Kate is welcomed back to fill her rightful position as the only Mrs. Clephane. This call homewards occasions, then, the rebirth of Kate as mother to Anne, the daughter she had " 'lost' " (16), the daughter against whom "she had barricaded her heart" (9). To reposition herself as mother, Kate must maneuver a treacherous path, described repeatedly in the novel as that on the verge of the abyss, between brutal self-honesty and self-effacement. At first she must finally admit to herself her willing desertion of her child so that she could "breathe" rather than be suffocated by "the thick atmosphere of self-approval and unperceivingness which emanated from John Clephane like coal-gas from a leaking furnace" (16); yet, she must also efface every detail of her life consequent to that act, even that which gave her a "real self," in order to be reborn as mother, awakened from her life among the ghosts, as Wharton's image of "the cable in her hand a cock-crow" suggests (10). That image also intimates, of course, that a betrayal has taken place, and one recognizes only at the end that this is the betrayal of that "real self" which had "cost" Kate so much (18).

One intuits as well from the outset the impossibility of Kate's reinstatement as mother. On first meeting Anne, she sees only her own "whole youth, her whole married past, in that small pale oval" (36); she recognizes Anne only as something in herself and not, as Anne stresses later, as her own person. Later on Kate searches in vain for the child she left behind, "the round child's body she had so long continued to feel against her own, like a warmth and an ache, as the amputated feel the life in a lost limb" (37). As Wharton's language here indicates, Kate has irrevocably lost contact with Anne and has been damaged permanently in that she has also lost her relationship to her mother self and now can only pretend to be a mother. Maintaining that pretense, as we learn in the novel, is exceedingly wearying. Further, "their so different pasts" (44) oppress Kate who repeatedly senses that "the abyss of all she didn't know about her daughter had once more opened before her" (42). Negotiating her passage on the verge of this abyss, as the mother encamped in the visitor's suite, as the outcast suddenly embraced by her judges, is "all too be-

wildering for a poor exile to come to terms with" (67). As Kate
seems incapable of finding herself in this new old world, Anne
proves to be the one most mother-like; she continually attempts
to assuage Kate's fears, to assure her with offers of security and
unquestioning love. In response, Kate is "frightened"; she cannot position herself as mother to such a "perfect" daughter,
perhaps because such perfection throws harsh light on her original inadequacy as a mother (45). There is also no need for her
to act as mother. As Anne makes clear in a remark to her guardian, she is "not a handful now to any one but myself—I'm in my
own hands" (38).

Kate's search for subject position as mother is not, however,
the major conflict of the novel. Instead, Wharton incorporates
a perversely modern twist to this family romance, one that has
already been suggested in her earlier portrayals of tribal New
York based on intermarriage between relations. Kate's young
lover, Chris Fenno, who awakened her "real self," is also reborn,
this time as Anne's fiancé and later husband. This incestuous
triangle foregrounds the irreconcilable dilemma which originally
confronts Kate on her return: to be a mother is to abjure self;
to desire selfhood is to abnegate motherhood. Kate can conceal
her past and prove a bad, duplicitous mother, or she can reveal
her affair and prove a good mother, albeit one who then destroys
her daughter's happiness. There is no way, however, that she
can position herself as both self and mother, since for mother
and daughter, each then becomes 'the other woman,' a transformation that would if made known necessarily destroy the
tenuous maternal relationship they have attempted to resurrect.
That Wharton's main interest lies in the incest theme is clear
from her letter to John Hugh Smith:

I felt, in writing it, all the force of what you say about the incest-element,
& its importance in justifying her anguish—but I felt it wd be hardly
visible in its exact sense to *her* [Kate], & wanted to try to represent the
business as it seemed to her, culminating in the incest-vision when she
sees the man holding Anne in his arms. (*Letters* 480)

It is also clear in the repeated scenes in which Kate thinks of
Anne and Chris at the same time and in the same way. Her

dilemma is not simply that she is "jealous of her daughter" (279), which feeling she finally admits to and flees from as "some incestuous horror" (279). More importantly, it is that she herself desires possession of Anne's desire—Chris, to be sure, as embodiment of that desire but also Anne's ability to desire and to be desired, or, perhaps in an even more incestuous reading, possession of Anne herself, who awakens Kate's deep passion for "possessing Anne's heart" (242). This last level of incestuous desire is, no doubt, that which Wharton refers to in her letter as the element "hardly visible" to Kate but crucial to Kate's final renunciation.

In the end, Kate acts out the part of the good enough mother, to use a contemporary label, or of "the 'good sort' of woman," to use Wharton's. She insures her daughter's happiness at the cost of her own in that she cedes her position of lover to her younger rival, her daughter Anne, and sacrifices motherhood by another self-banishment in order that her daughter and her life remain "perfect." In short, Kate visits the maternal sphere but finds no place in it for her self precisely because a mother is denied a self, a past, or a desire beyond that of maternal love. Wharton at one early point of the novel offers us the deeply alienated image of Kate within Anne's group "hugging her new self in her anxious arms, turning its smooth face toward them, and furtively regulating its non-committal gestures and the sounds that issued from its lips" (136). She has been reborn as a schizophrenic mating of ventriloquist and dummy, the former a slave to her audience, the latter an even more disturbing image of Kate's self-manipulation and compromise. To be a mother to a high-born New York girl is to become, as Kate calls another character, merely a "scrupulous social puppet" (245).

What betrayal occurs, then, if Kate proves in the end to be a good enough mother, a good sort of woman? Elizabeth Ammons reads the novel's ending, in which Kate also banishes the possibility of consolation through marriage to Fred Landers, as Wharton's approval of Kate's "abnegation and self-punishment," "the mother's recompense for abandoning her child and leading a promiscuous life." Ammons also argues, however, that Wharton betrays her own creation, that because "the subject of mothers who refuse to mother blinds Wharton," the writer "sacrifices

Kate as a person to her theoretical preoccupation with Kate the mother" (163). This argument relies on Ammon's earlier assertion that for Wharton, in her last novels, "women are meant to be mothers" (162). Such a reading reflects, perhaps, too much the dilemma which Kate confronts just as it misinterprets, as Kate does, her position as one of open possibilities—that Kate might be both mother and herself, that her two lives, each speaking a different type of desire, might coexist and inform one another. Ammons' analysis is certainly acute in part. One does see, for instance, the old betrayal between parent and child, each loving the other too much in too particular and limited a way so that individuation, self-differentiation, proves impossible. Kate herself senses betrayal in her double act of deserting Anne, once when she is a child and the last time when she gives her to Chris at the altar. Perhaps this, too, is but another version of the parent's woe—sending one's beloved and defenseless child out into "a world such as she now knew it to be" (159). Kate also speaks, however, of "self-betrayal" (151), alluding to her fear of the consequences if she reveal her past. One might argue that the reader's understanding of that "self-betrayal" surpasses Kate's by the end of the novel. It is, of course, crucial to recall that her descent into incestuous passion is forced on her: it is not she who steals her daughter's lover; it is not she who seeks reinstatement as the mother figure. Further, in Kate's descent into the abyss of incestuous passion, an abyss in which she finds herself appallingly alone, repugnant to "the tribal eye" (254) and to her own narcissistic gaze, she loses that self which originally gave meaning to her life. The tragedy, and Wharton expected her readers would understand that the novel did end "tragically" (*Letters* 483), is that there is no help for this self-loss, no possible recompense for the self-renunciation exacted by unrequitable desires beyond that of the knowledge that one has faced the incomprehensible and absorbed it into one's self. Kate gives her daughter to her lover, rejects the possibility of consolation in her own marriage, and reestablishes herself in the Riviera demimonde as if she has "simply turned back a chapter, and begun again at the top of the same dull page" (328). Yet, like Newland Archer, she at least knows that she has loved without causing "sterile pain" (266):

Nothing on earth would ever again help her—help to blot out the old horrors and the new loneliness—as much as the fact of being able to take her stand on that resolve, of being able to say to herself, whenever she began to drift toward new uncertainties and fresh concessions, that once at least she had stood fast, shutting away in a little space of peace and light the best thing that had ever happened to her. (342)

That her act of love—for Chris, Anne, Fred, herself—is at the cost of the many selves which give meaning to her life—as lover and beloved, as mother and wife—is the tragedy of the mother's recompense. As is the case of Newland in *The Age of Innocence*, for Kate, the sole consolation is the "desolation" with which Wharton encloses her story (*Letters* 483). As a modern reading of desire and abjection, *The Mother's Recompense* deserves serious critical reevaluation.

Such a case can also be made for Wharton's next two novels, *Twilight Sleep* (1927) and *The Children* (1928), the latter her most successful bestseller. They are not, to be sure, works equal in sustained control of style and content to that in *The Age of Innocence* or *The Custom of the Country* and are in fact heavily indebted to those works both for general themes and specific set pieces. They do, however, extend the very complicated reading of desire set out in *The Glimpses of the Moon* and *The Mother's Recompense*. That the 1920 novels are problematic in their preoccupation with perversely alienated desire was clear to Wharton herself. As Wharton makes clear in a letter to Margaret Terry Chanler, she was deeply affected by the negative or misinformed reviews her late works received and had begun as early as 1925 to question her own ability to relay the messages she deemed central in her novels: "as my work reaches its close, I feel so sure that it is either nothing, or far more than they know.... And I wonder, a little desolately, which?" (483). Here she consciously echoes the language which opens *The Mother's Recompense*, the epigram "Desolation is a delicate thing." It is ironic, then, that though her own sense of wonder and doubt might be delicate, her next novel, *Twilight Sleep* be perceived (and perhaps conceived) as an extremely bold "indictment of our ghastly age of Fordian culture" (*Letters* 547).

The novel, highly reminiscent of the satiric *The Custom of the*

Country, furthers Wharton's critique of self-alienation enacted within the familial or private sphere. We are first presented with the perfect modern mother who advocates the "twilight sleep" of painless childbirth as well as "Birth Control and unlimited maternity, free love or the return to the traditions of the American home" (5), that home transformed into "the perfect establishment" (13) in which children must make appointments to see their parents. The children themselves belong "to another generation: to the bewildered disenchanted young people who had grown up since the Great War, whose energies were more spasmodic and less definitely directed, and who, above all, wanted a more personal outlet for them" (6–7). In this industrial state in which babies are "something to be turned out in series like Fords" (15) by unconscious, benumbed mothers and in which people's lives are regularly "disinfected and whitewashed" (19), the expression of individual desire is even more problematic than for Kate in *The Mother's Recompense*. Again, desire appears most climactically in its incestuous form—here a man's desire for his stepson's wife. Wharton's continued focus on such outré incestuous relationships, begun long before in *Summer*, suggests her belief that the loss which desire seeks to redress is that of family. Incest seems to promise the most intimate of familial relationships, ironically so in its eradication of generational difference. It is also, however, one of the most forbidden acts of "union" in that in its eradication of difference, it destroys the family in which it is enacted. Loss of family, both the loss occasioned by modern redefinitions of the relationships which obtain between family members and the relationships which some family members seek as compensation, is the most profound occasion of despair for Wharton's modern Americans. While the old codes preserved family at the cost of individual self-fulfillment, the new lack of codes results in a splintering of both self and family, a chaotic multiplication of loss, the sterile pain that Kate in *The Mother's Recompense* fears.

The novel reads, in fact, as a catalogue of losses, its world one of ennui, indifference, or sterile efficiency counterposed to one recreated from evanescent memories or visions of a life—usually set in the countryside—in which deep, lasting relationships are the norm as are the old virtues of honor, fidelity, and compassion. The father figure Dexter Manford, for example, first dreams of a simple life on the land with Lilla, his stepson's wife, and only later surrenders that to a vision of the immediate pleasure her body promises. Similarly, his daughter Nona consoles herself with childhood memories of prelapsarian scenes of innocent pleasure with her stepbrother in the woods. Such evasions are necessary to them, for, as Nona feels it, life has become a constant war zone, a no man's land across which one must watch unceasingly for the forever unseen enemy. She also believes, however, that one watches so long that one inevitably falls prey to daydreams; one then becomes so entranced by visions of a golden world so that in a moment of inattention to reality, one is destroyed. Many critics have argued that this novel, and the post–1920 works as a whole, indicate Wharton's reactionary response to the lost generation, the flapper era, the modern world. Nona's belief, however, opposes such a critique, and Nona is clearly one of the few characters in this novel with whom Wharton sympathizes. While Wharton clearly satirizes modern excesses, especially the narcissistic pursuit of eternal youth and the commercialization of religion and art, she is also just as pointedly criticizing a purely looking-backward philosophy of life, the reliance on evanescent memories or dreams as escape from reality. In such a society in which love always proves traumatic or severely compromised, there is a great need, Wharton suggests, for a new ethics or code of honor, perhaps one based in part on the old code. We see this both in the dreams of those who still desire—Nona, her father, her stepfather, her stepbrother—and in the actions which their pursuit of desire effect.

For instance, Nona is accidentally shot when she comes between her father, her stepfather, and her stepsister-in-law, absorbing within herself symbolically the incestuous horror which threatens to rip her extended family apart. She does this partly because of her deep love for her stepbrother, a purified version of incestuous desire, but primarily because, as she says, " 'I do believe . . . I know most of the new ways of being rotten; I only wish I was sure I knew the best new way of being decent . . . ' " (244). Despite her desire for a new ethics of being, hers is not a sacrifice which brings happiness, even though it serves the immediate purpose of reconstituting traditional familial rela-

tionships. Her act is futile precisely because she only feels desire
for a new way of being but cannot articulate this need to others
or, even, adequately to herself. Further, though she finally espies
and confronts the enemy traversing a noman's land of desire,
she is also wounded in the act. Her only ally is her alcoholic stepfather whom she calls throughout the novel Exhibit A. They are
both but objects which temporarily obstruct the process of social
disintegration, symbolized by the incestuous affair. Her stepfather is erased from the text after his one ethical act, his attempt
for the sake of his son to disrupt incestuous coupling. For her
part, Nona is less physically damaged than she is psychically. At
the end of the novel, she seeks only escape into solitude, self-
loss in a reclusive abyss "where nobody believes in anything"
(373). Her desire and her blind act of interference do not lead
to growth in consciousness or a final call for ethics to counteract
despair.

The extremely confusing confrontation scene moves the
reader to question the identity of the enemy and the efficacy of
ethical behavior in the face of indifference, willful blindness, or
perverse desire. One is frustrated, as is Nona, in the attempt to
make meaning out of such chaos masquerading as progress or
'simple' pleasure. If the enemy be desire as transgression which
all share but most repress, as Nona does, the "war" then becomes
internalized with no clear victory possible. If the enemy be the
twilight sleep of the modern world in which all drift "unper-
ceivingly" (14), then the only measures possible are forms of self-
surrender. Nona's fear of "falling asleep," of "losing" herself "in
waking dreams" (280), recalls the words of Edna Pontellier, another who suffers the aftereffects of twilight sleep: " 'Yes,' she
said. 'The years that are gone seem like dreams—if one might
go on sleeping and dreaming—but to wake up and find—oh!
well! perhaps it is better to wake up after all, even to suffer,
rather than to remain a dupe to illusions all one's life' " (996).
Perhaps what critics misread in these works as Wharton's reactionary response to modernity is in fact her ineluctably bleak
vision of the coming universal alienation, what Thomas Hardy
called "the ache of modernism," "the beginning of the coming
universal wish not to live" (*Tess* 160, *Jude* 406).

In this novel, one also sees that Wharton's work shares the

central concerns that we identify with modernism, those that inform the works of, for instance, T. S. Eliot or of Aldous Huxley, who called *Twilight Sleep* the novel that had done all of *Brave New World* before he wrote it (*Letters* 547). Her work is distinguished, however, by its preoccupation with incest as the modern form of desire. In her continued reliance on incest as central plot motivation, she offers the most basic of tribal taboos as a shocking but perversely comprehensible response to the individual fear of the abyss. Even the pre–1920 works prefigure this focus with their central portrayals of the New York 400 and the nearly incestuous marriages which preserve that society in its exclusivity or of the Starkfield/North Dormer communities in which the too-close bonds within families result in grievous injury, self-capitulation, or death (and Wharton makes a very dark joke, indeed, by positioning the communities of *Ethan Frome* and *Summer* uncomfortably close to the poisonously named Hemlock County of the vampiric "Bewitched"). Incest is, as has been argued, a desire doomed by its very transgressive nature in that in its eradication of familial difference, it destroys the family. We see this in the unbreachable distance between family members at the conclusion of *The Mother's Recompense* and of *Twilight Sleep*, the family members fleeing to different corners of the globe in order to maintain the illusion of family unity. And in Nona's case, the self seems to have been destroyed by this mockery of what still holds meaning for her. As Nona feared, such a world sacrifices its children to the pursuit of unthinking pleasure:

the demons the elder generation ignored, baulked of their natural prey, had cast their hungry shadow over the young. After all, somebody in every family had to remember now and then that such things as wickedness, suffering and death had not yet been banished from the earth; ... perhaps their children had to serve as vicarious sacrifices. There were hours when Nona Manford, bewildered little Iphigenia, uneasily argued in this way. (47–48)

Wharton's invention in this novel of desire enacted solely through incest is, then, her modernist portrayal of the "massacre of innocents" (211) to "the powers of darkness" (48). The old sacrifice of Lily Bart to the ways of the tribe has been grotesquely transformed, multiplied, in this more modern world into the sacrifice of all children at the hands of parents. Wharton's work in this light evokes the highly disturbing vision of the death of the future.

Twilight Sleep does not, however, end Wharton's analysis of incestuous desire. Wharton was aware that incest promises more than recuperation of a lost or idealized past in intense intimacy. It also seems to offer, in these cross-generational couplings, the promise of new beginnings for the parental figure, for Kate her "real self," for Nona's father, "immediate satisfaction" and "animal sincerity" (190) free of agendas or the sense of duty. Such cross-generational couples are, as well, a perversely "natural" response as one sees in *The Children* (1928), which focuses on a society in which families are made obsolete by divorce and in which the parents prove more immature than the children.

The Children presents yet another quasi-incestuous relationship, here one between a middle-aged man and a fifteen-year-old girl who treats him as a father. In her he seeks the eternal feminine, the girl-mother who represents both "excessive youth and a rather pathetic grace" (4). Again, Judith Wheater, like Nona, is a girl forced too soon to become a woman, an innocent sacrificed to her parents' pursuit of pleasure. She acts as mother to six children born of her parents' various liaisons, kidnapping them at one point in a futile attempt to keep them together as one family protected by her love from the "wilderness," "the world *we* live in" (23). Martin Boyne, a man with "twilight gray" eyes (3), idealizes her in ways similar to the forms of male objectification of women seen in all of Wharton's works; he sees her not as an individual invested with complicated and contradictory desires and needs but as he needs to see her, as helpless, incomplete, reliant on him for his superior wisdom, strength, and position, as a reflection of his male desire:

"A strange little creature who changes every hour, hardly seems to have any personality of her own except when she's mothering her flock. Then she's extraordinary: playmate, mother and governess all in one; and the best of each in its way. As for her very self, when she's not with them, you grope for her identity and find an instrument the wind plays on, a looking-glass that reflects the clouds, a queer little sensitive plate, very little and very sensitive." (37)

She awakens his desire in several ways, most of which he never fully comprehends.

One of his desires is that of escaping mature attachment, in his case to the woman he has supposedly loved for years, Rose Sellars, who is now free to marry him. Rose symbolizes for him mature love, social conformity, his own middle age. He alternately thinks of her as an angel or as a ghost but not, but for brief moments of near intimacy, as a flesh and blood woman. Judith, in contrast, is "warm animal life," as Lilla was for Dexter Manford (45). It is a life which he himself seems to have lost in his self-alienation, in his twilight gray sleep. One understands well his desire for Judith; one also sees the evasive and self-delusory element of his relationship to her.

Martin's primary desire, however, is for Judith, not only for what she symbolizes but also for her incomplete self and her body. After their chance meeting, he becomes hopelessly enmeshed in her struggle to save her family of children, and her reliance on him as the only responsible and sympathetic authority figure she knows throws them together continually in a most intimate way. Her own desire is focused solely on preserving "her" children's collectivity, and in her battle to do so, she opens herself completely to Martin, confiding in him, exposing herself. And she is an artless child-woman, alternately entrancing and utterly naive. It is not surprising that Martin in his flight from what Rose represents—capitulation to social conformity, utter self-composure, "Logic" (172)—responds to Judith and the other children as he does. While he remains a responsible adult for most of the novel in his guardianship of them, he does so not primarily because of a sense of duty but because they reflect his own undeveloped self: "he suspected that, even had their plight not roused his pity, his own restlessness and impulsiveness would have fraternized with theirs. 'The fact is, we're none of us grown up,' he reflected, hugging himself for being on the children's side of the eternal barrier" (247). Like Eliot's Prufrock, he wishes one last time to hear the siren call, to wade childlike in the sea of desire, to taste that sweet and pure desire.

The novel does not, however, merely portray one man's quest for a second childhood. Instead, it is Martin's other desire—for Judith as lover and wife—that is *The Children*'s most involving story. Martin himself denies such a desire for much of his time with the children, a denial maintained in the face of others' realization of his love for Judith. Rose names his desire at one point but then backs away from a confrontation over what should be an unimaginable occurrence. Martin also evades self-realization, projecting in one scene his desire for Judith into another even older man's gaze. He sees Rose's lawyer staring at a sleeping, and thus defenseless, Judith and is repulsed by the lust he imagines in the other man's look (206). While he briefly wonders whether Dobree is "serving as his mirror," he shies away from such self-exploration, "frightened at himself" (206). Wharton emphasizes how distant he is from self-recognition in her last picture of him in this scene. Left alone with Judith, he gazes at her sandalled feet: "For the moment his imagination was imprisoned in a circle close about them" (211). He has surrendered self-consciousness to fetishism, a willful self-entrapment by and perversion of his own desire.

It is only at the end of the novel that Martin admits his need for Judith, what he calls "madness" (307), only at the point when his "golden" world (304) has begun to disintegrate. He breaks with Rose over his involvement with the children, yet that involvement proves futile as the various parents (or their new spouses) assert claims to their particular children. He then offers Judith one last chance—their marriage—to keep them all together, a proposal which disguises again in its intention his primary desire. Judith misinterprets him completely in that she believes he means to adopt them, not that he is proposing marriage to her. In that one moment of misprision, he faces the abyss: "Boyne felt like a man who has blundered along in the dark to the edge of a precipice" (310).

Again, the promise of new beginnings proves delusive, not because such is punishment for the sin of desire (the quasi-incestuous passion Martin feels for Judith) but because any desire for self-realization and union with another, located in these late works in the incestuous impulse, seems to be either forbidden or silenced by those maintaining the old way—Nona's step-

father and Nona herself, Rose Sellars—or is no longer comprehensible to the new society whose members have become as two-
dimensional in their relationships as are the lovers on the silver
screen Wharton so often disparages. One sees this clearly in
Twilight Sleep's Manfords, the old patriarchal code of Man conjoined with the sterile maternity/modernity of Ford. Wharton
seems to suggest that in this modern world there is no longer a
language, except the perverse or the repressed, which can express self-desire. In *The Children*, for instance, Martin cannot for
a long time articulate his desire even to himself; further, when
the crucial moment arises, he cannot speak clearly to Judith. He
also cannot bridge the abyss between them, the disparity between
their desires, hers for a community of the future—the children,
his for union with her, escape from "the empty present" (333).
They are both in the end lost to the twilight modern world, "the
gray curtain of failure" descending upon them (304). In a scene
highly reminiscent of *The Age of Innocence*'s conclusion, Martin
returns after three years of self-exile and escape through good
work only to confront again, as Newland did, the one desire
which gave him intense pleasure as well as pain. He learns that
the children have separated, the baby has died, that Judith—
though surrounded by admirers—is still alone. He goes to find
her. Martin then stands outside a ballroom in which Judith
dances, dressed in a gown glazed with silver, the rain blowing
in his face so that "he might almost have fancied he was crying"
(345). He gazes at her with his twilight gray eyes and for the
first time sees her singular self: " '*Judith*!' Boyne thought; as if
her being Judith, her being herself, were impossible to believe,
yet too sweet for anything else in the world to be true." He also
realizes that her life is lost to him, that "he would never know"
her or fully understand his desire for her (347). In an earlier
scene, Judith and the children presented him with "an ancient
walnut cradle with primitive carven ornaments" (255), a wedding
present intended for Martin and Rose. That gift is an extremely
complex symbol in that it reflects his denial of sexuality with
Rose with whom he has already broken, Judith's own naive sexuality and relationship to him, and Martin's fear of sexuality
with Judith, suggested by his "petrified gaze" upon the cradle
(255). It is also his own cradle, at first desecrated by Martin who

uses it to hold his boots, an act suggestive of his trampling down his desire. Later, like Chopin's Edna, he is reborn through desire but torments himself in its misuse. Even more painfully, his awakening remains self-contained, comprehensible at last only to himself. Also like Edna, he returns to the sea and to self-exile, to the abyss of solitude. His loss at the end again bespeaks the modern condition: "When two people part who have loved each other it is as if what happens between them befell in a great emptiness—as if the tearing asunder of the flesh must turn at last into a disembodied anguish" (323).

Wharton's final and most striking example of perverse desire and "disembodied anguish" is, of course, the "Beatrice Palmato" fragment, dated 1935, her pornographic description of intercourse between father and daughter after the daughter's unhappy marriage, the consummation of their incestuous relationship begun when Beatrice was a child. Wharton's writing here is both graphic and seductive; in this piece, a woman's erotic pleasure is breathtakingly portrayed. Whatever her reasons for writing and preserving this text, one sees that Wharton knows intimately the language of the perverse, the language which her novel characters cannot articulate, as well as its dangerous possibilities for transgressing all boundaries. Beatrice's father speaks their desire, and she falls into "new abysses of bliss" (Lewis *Edith Wharton* 548). What is most striking about the fragment, however, is that it transgresses even the boundaries of Wharton's projected piece. In the outline accompanying it, one finds no place for the fragment, indeed no place for pleasure. Instead, the story is one of child abuse, the father's sexual use of the children leading to the elder daughter's suicide, the mother's descent into madness and death in an asylum, Beatrice's own suicide after her unwitting exposure to her husband of her traumatic incestuous experience. The fragment even in what R.W.B. Lewis calls its "well-rehearsed ritualistic quality" (524) suggests again the sacrifice of a child to a parent's desire. Beatrice lies down before the fire and sees literally for the first time the reality to which her father has made her complicit. That she is satisfied beyond measure is Wharton's fantasy and frisson, her last assault on the ultimate taboo. That Beatrice must suffer and die in the story after confronting her husband over his affection for their daughter (born of her father) is Wharton's most chilling account of the cost of such desire.

Perhaps this unfinished work suggests, then, along with the late novels, that for Wharton all desire had been perverted by the acts of fathers and mothers, the authority figures who themselves seem grotesquely incapable of sublimation, of a social consciousness. One might believe that Wharton had come to feel that self-desire and desire for desire had become pornographic. Indeed, in these last works, the life of the soul and self is psychotically sterilized or eroticized, the world become a barren wasteland between the wars to which parents sacrifice children. One might also contemplate whether Wharton's final transgression, her pornographic ace pulled out from up her sleeve (*Letters* 589), is not her most radical social critique. As Susan Sontag writes in "The Pornographic Imagination," critics of pornography continuously overlook the profound pathos it bespeaks, a pathos in response "to something more general than even sexual damage":

I mean the traumatic failure of modern capitalist society to provide authentic outlets for the perennial human flair for high-temperature visionary obsessions, to satisfy the appetite for exalted self-transcending modes of concentration and seriousness. The need of human beings to transcend "the personal" is no less profound than the need to be a person, an individual. But this society serves that need poorly. It provides mainly demonic vocabularies in which to situate that need and from which to initiate action and construct rites of behavior. One is offered a choice among vocabularies of thought and action which are not merely self-transcending but self-destructive. (70)

To read the pathos in Wharton's work is to acknowledge what is being mourned as well as what is being celebrated. Within the world she creates for us, a world mirroring that in which we live, self-transcendence through transgression is too often an obscene distortion of that same old story, the one in which cycles of abuse result in self-annihilation. In her major works, the characters who survive do so not in abysses of bliss. For Wharton, as is true for Chopin as well, the desire for liminality and for autonomy remains always a double bind to which seemingly the only responses possible are ambivalence, stoicism, profound alienation.

As Wharton wrote in her autobiographical *A Backward Glance*, "The welter is always there, and the present generation hears close underfoot the growling of the volcano on which ours danced so long; but in our individual lives, though the years are sad, the days have a way of being jubilant. Life is the saddest thing there is, next to death" (379).

7

Afterword

Edith Wharton wrote in her private diary: " 'Life is always either a tight-rope or a feather bed. Give me the tight-rope!' " (Wolff, *Feast* 344). She and Chopin both challenged others to make the same choice, to traverse the abysses of solitude or despair rather than to settle into the social bed of conformity and complacency. In their last works, they continued to seek avenues of self-fulfillment as well as sources of consolation to offer those struggling against self-loss.

After completing *The Awakening*, Chopin did not surrender her individual voice to the vox populi. Like Wharton, she carried forward her analysis of social conditions and conditioning while simultaneously evoking one last radical vision of what she termed "the living spirit." Those stories are not always successful syntheses of social critique and art, yet one stands out as remarkable.

In "The Storm," written 19 July 1898 and never published in Chopin's lifetime, an explicitly sexual awakening occurs: the rekindled desires of the two lovers whom Chopin had portrayed in her earlier "At the 'Cadian Ball" are consummated in an act of adultery. Although the tale recounts an intensely sensual encounter, Chopin here does not compromise her characters by burdening them with blind passion; neither does she lessen their shared experience by giving them at the end negative self-consciousness. Instead, the lovers part, then reunite by word or deed with their families, and all live happily ever after. Alcée and Calixta are shown as equals in desire and self-desire; their union is both self-revelation and perfect duality. In "The Storm," then, Chopin makes an astounding leap of faith: in this work, the search for selfhood and the satisfaction of desire are presented as part of a possible and positive process, despite what the social and moral commandments say. The "abyss of solitude" is no longer even a remote threat in the new world born of Calixta and Alcée and then carried forth to others.

While "The Storm" is Chopin's most radical vision, it is also her last piece which truly dares and defies. As Helen Taylor writes, *The Awakening* and this story "were the logical conclusion of all Chopin's writing about women. Both celebrate woman as an infinitely desiring and versatile subject, and both demonstrate the power of erotic bliss in the creation of a new kind of woman" (202). After writing these works, however, Chopin seemed to foresee the approaching critical debacle. Her unpublished poem entitled "The Haunted Chamber," written in February 1899 just before the novel's publication, painfully conceals, in its use of a male narrator, and reveals, in its subject matter, her own consciousness and self-will. In this work, a man tells of "a fair, frail, passionate woman who fell," whose story is to the men hearing it "more of a joke / Than a matter of sin or a matter of shame." The woman's suffering is initially discounted until the narrator, once alone, hears her "far, faint voice" on the wind arising from abysmal "depths of some infinite gloom." This voice torments him in its inarticulateness, in its pure misery. At the end, however, he again attempts to shrug it off, saying, "But women forever will whine and cry / And men forever must listen—and sigh—" (733–734). This poem suggests, then, that Chopin did not kill her art after *The Awakening*, as so many critics would have it; she thereafter merely muted her voice in order that her own words might perhaps be heard. That voice still calls to us.

Wharton also continued to produce almost until her dying breath. Like Chopin's final lines, Wharton's last major works offer visions of bliss and despair. She too had always found solace in work and had given this source of consolation to some loved characters: Newland Archer in *The Age of Innocence* and Martin Boyne in *The Children* preserve themselves, however damaged they may be, through surrendering self-interest to social work. Similarly, John Campton, the portrait painter in *A Son At the Front*, finds self-purpose through his art, as do Chopin's Paula Von Stoltz and Mademoiselle Reisz. In *Hudson River Bracketed* and *The Gods Arrive*, Wharton explores further the realm and responsibilities of the artist as well as the business of literature which can pervert artistic creation, stripping it of its singular expressiveness. Like Chopin's Edna Pontellier, Wharton's Vance Weston returns again and again to the sea, the source of his inspiration, "this expanse which rested not yet moved not, except in a rhythmic sway as regular as the march of the heavens" (*Hudson* 180). A writer like Chopin and Wharton, he searches for an aesthetic of "ecstasy," that which because it is " 'true of life' " should be " 'true of art' " as well (*Letters* 388). He fails miserably precisely because he cannot incorporate "the living spirit" into "the dead letter" of his fiction or into his relationships with women. He does not, like Wharton, know "the gods" the moment he meets them (*Letters* 604). Unlike Weston, Wharton to the end did not surrender her ecstatic sense of life's possibilities. She wrote to Mary Berenson, "I wish I knew what people mean when they say they find 'emptiness' in this wonderful adventure of living, which seems to me to pile up its glories like an horizon-wide sunset as the light declines. I'm afraid I'm an incorrigible life-lover & life-wonderer & adventurer" (*Letters* 598). Her last novel, *The Buccaneers*, left unfinished at her death, speaks once more of such an adventurer as well as of the promise that one might find communion with one other solitary soul. Laura Testvalley's story of unconventional yet uncompromised love had the makings of another storm.

Yet Wharton also never deafened herself to the unspeakably sad stories of women who can do nothing but "whine and cry." Her "Miss Mary Pask" (1925) recalls to us Chopin's "The Haunted Chamber." In this short story a man meets what he believes at first to be the ghost of Mary Pask and then is horrified to discover her dead life, one in which she could find no other in whom to reflect herself, no other one to love her and to love. He speaks, as Chopin's narrator does, for her:

Supposing something survived of Mary Pask—enough to cry out to me the unuttered loneliness of a lifetime, to express at last what the living woman had always had to keep dumb and hidden? The thought moved me curiously—in my weakness I lay and wept over it. No end of women were like that, I supposed, and perhaps, after death, if they got their chance they tried to use it. (*Stories* II, 382)

So Wharton's women haunt us, their voices like those of Chopin's women constantly murmuring, inviting us to reflect for a spell upon those moments when language proves inadequate, beyond the order of the text.

Wharton's narrator in *Ethan Frome* says, "Though Harmon Gow developed the tale as far as his mental and moral reach permitted there were perceptible gaps between his facts, and I had the sense that the deeper meaning of the story was in the gaps" (7). Chopin and Wharton both move us repeatedly to seek out those deeper meanings in their stories, to see beyond the set lines. What cannot be articulated—female desire, self-desire—becomes then as crucial as what is said—the account of woman's reality, the larger world view and social critique. Such radical visions bespeak radical criticism, and it is time to take up Chopin's challenge to dare and defy as well as Wharton's dare of walking the literary and social tight-rope above the safe net of traditional beliefs. We must hear these works and then do more than just sigh. Taking up these radical writers before us, we must at last speak the unspeakable to each other and thus transform abysses of solitude into an uprising of individual response and collective responsibility. In this way we might make every thing new. Christa Wolf writes, "Paradise can make itself scarce, that's the way of it. Make a wry face if you like, but all the same: one must, once in a lifetime, when the time is right, have believed in the impossible" (52). It is precisely that belief in the seemingly impossible—the unfixing of authority, the articulation of desire—that we find cast in negative in the works of Chopin and Wharton. Their words recall us to moments when such a belief began and help to keep that belief alive while it is still in the process of coming to be in ourselves and in our world.

Bibliography

PRIMARY SOURCES

Chopin, Kate. *The Complete Works of Kate Chopin*. Edited and with an Introduction by Per Seyersted. Foreword by Edmund Wilson. Baton Rouge: Louisiana State University Press, 1969. (Includes besides unpublished material: *At Fault*. St. Louis: Nixon-Jones Printing Co., 1890; *Bayou Folk*. Boston: Houghton Mifflin & Co., 1894; *A Night in Acadie*. Chicago: Way & Williams, 1897; *The Awakening*. Chicago and New York: Herbert S. Stone and Co., 1899.)

————. *A Kate Chopin Miscellany*. Edited and with a Preface by Per Seyersted; Emily Toth, assistant editor. Natchitoches: Northwestern State University Press, 1979.

Wharton, Edith. *The Age of Innocence*. New York: D. Appleton and Company, 1920; New York: Charles Scribner's Sons, 1970.

————. An Autobiographical Postscript. *The Ghost Stories of Edith Wharton*. New York: Charles Scribner's Sons, 1973. 275–276.

————. *A Backward Glance*. New York: D. Appleton-Century Company, Inc., 1934.

————. *The Buccaneers*. New York: Appleton-Century, 1938.

————. *Certain People*. New York: D. Appleton & Co., 1930.

————. *The Children*. New York: D. Appleton & Co., 1928.

————. *The Collected Short Stories of Edith Wharton*. Two volumes. Edited by R.W.B. Lewis. New York: Charles Scribner's Sons, 1968.

————. "Confessions of a Novelist." *The Atlantic Monthly* 151.4 (April 1933): 385–392.

————. "The Criticism of Fiction." *Times Literary Supplement* 643 (14 May 1914): 229–230.

————. *Crucial Instances*. New York: Charles Scribner's Sons, 1901.

————. *The Custom of the Country*. New York: Charles Scribner's Sons, 1913.

————. "A Cycle of Reviewing." *Spectator* 141 (3 November 1928): supplement pages 44–45.

————. *The Descent of Man, and Other Stories*. New York: Charles Scribner's Sons, 1904.

————. *Ethan Frome*. New York: Charles Scribner's Sons, 1911 and 1970.

————. *Fast and Loose: A Novelette by David Olivieri*. Edited by Viola Hopkins Winner. Charlottesville: University Press of Virginia, 1977.

————. *Fighting France from Dunkerque to Belfort*. New York: Charles Scribner's Sons, 1915.

————. *French Ways and Their Meaning*. New York: D. Appleton and Company, 1919.

————. *The Fruit of the Tree*. New York: Charles Scribner's Sons, 1907.

————. *Ghosts*. New York: Appleton-Century, 1937.

————. *The Glimpses of the Moon*. New York: D. Appleton & Co., 1922.

————. *The Gods Arrive*. New York: D. Appleton & Co., 1932.

————. "The Great American Novel." *Yale Review* n.s. 16 (July 1927): 646–656.

————. *The Greater Inclination*. New York: Charles Scribner's Sons, 1899.

————. "Henry James in his Letters." *The Quarterly Review* 234.464 (July 1920): 188–202.

————. *Here and Beyond*. New York: D. Appleton & Co., 1926.

————. *The Hermit and the Wild Woman, and Other Stories*. New York: Charles Scribner's Sons, 1908.

————. *The House of Mirth*. New York: Charles Scribner's Sons, 1905.

————. *Hudson River Bracketed*. New York: D. Appleton & Co., 1929.

————. *Human Nature*. New York: D. Appleton & Co., 1933.

————. *In Morocco*. New York: Charles Scribner's Sons, 1920.

————. Introduction. *Ethan Frome*. New York: Charles Scribner's Sons, 1922 and 1970. v-x.

————. Introduction. *The House of Mirth*. London: Oxford University Press, 1936. v-xi.

————. *Italian Backgrounds*. New York: Charles Scribner's Sons, 1905.

————. *Italian Villas and Their Gardens*. New York: The Century Co., 1904.

————. *The Letters of Edith Wharton*. Edited by R.W.B. Lewis, Nancy Lewis, and William R. Tyler. New York: Charles Scribner's Sons, 1988.

————. *Madame de Treymes*. New York: Charles Scribner's Sons, 1907.

———. *The Marne.* New York: D. Appleton and Company, 1918.

———. "More Love Letters of an Englishwoman." *Bookman* 12 (February 1901): 561–563.

———. *The Mother's Recompense.* New York: D. Appleton & Co., 1925.

———. *A Motor-Flight Through France.* New York: Charles Scribner's Sons, 1908.

———. *Old New York: False Dawn (The 'Forties); The Old Maid (The 'Fifties); The Spark (The 'Sixties); New Year's Day (The 'Seventies).* New York: D. Appleton & Co., 1924.

———. "Permanent Values in Fiction." *Saturday Review of Literature* 10.38 (7 April 1934): 603–604.

———. "A Reconsideration of Proust." *Saturday Review of Literature* 11.15 (27 October 1934): 233–234.

———. *The Reef.* New York: Charles Scribner's Sons, 1912.

———. Rev. of *George Eliot,* by Leslie Stephen. *Bookman* 15 (May 1902): 247–251.

———. Rev. of *The Fool Errant,* by Maurice Hewlett. *Bookman* 22 (September 1905): 64–67.

———. Rev. of *Belchamber,* by Mr. Sturgis. *Bookman* 21 (May 1905): 307–310.

———. *Sanctuary.* New York: Charles Scribner's Sons, 1903; Upper Saddle River, New Jersey: Gregg Press Literature House, 1970.

———. *A Son at the Front.* New York: Charles Scribner's Sons, 1923.

———. *Summer.* New York: D. Appleton and Co., 1917; Toronto: George J. McLeod, Limited, 1917.

———. *Tales of Men and Ghosts.* New York: Charles Scribner's Sons, 1910.

———. "Tendencies in Modern Fiction." *Saturday Review of Literature* 10.28 (27 January 1934): 433–434.

———. *The Touchstone.* New York: Charles Scribner's Sons, 1900; published in England as *A Gift from the Grave.* London: John Murray, 1900; Grosse Point: Scholarly Press, 1968.

———. *Twilight Sleep.* New York: D. Appleton & Co., 1928.

———. *The Valley of Decision.* Two volumes. New York: Charles Scribner's Sons, 1902.

———. "The Vice of Reading." *North American Review* 177.563 (October 1903): 513–521.

———. "Visibility in Fiction." *Yale Review* n.s. 18 (March 1929): 480–488.

———. *The World Over.* New York: Appleton-Century, 1936.

———. "The Writing of *Ethan Frome.*" *The Colophon: The Book Collectors' Quarterly,* pt. 11.4 (September 1932): n. pag.

————. *The Writing of Fiction*. New York: Charles Scribner's Sons, 1925.

————. *Xingu and Other Stories*. New York: Charles Scribner's Sons, 1916.

————, ed. *The Book of the Homeless (Le Livre des Sans-Foyer)*. New York and London: Macmillan & Co., Limited, 1916.

————, and Ogden Codman, Jr. *The Decoration of Houses*. New York: Charles Scribner's Sons, 1897.

SECONDARY SOURCES

Agonito, Rosemary. *History of Ideas on Woman: A Source Book*. New York: G. P. Putnam's Sons, 1977.

Ammons, Elizabeth. *Edith Wharton's Argument with America*. Athens: University of Georgia Press, 1980.

Arner, Robert. "Kate Chopin." *Louisiana Studies* 14.1 (Spring 1975): 11–139.

Auchincloss, Louis. Afterword. *The House of Mirth*. By Edith Wharton. New York: New American Library, 1964. 343–349.

————. *Edith Wharton*. Minneapolis: University of Minnesota Press, 1961.

————. *Edith Wharton: A Woman in Her Time*. New York: Viking Press, 1971.

————. "Edith Wharton and Her New Yorks." *Reflections of a Jacobite*. London: Victor Gollancz Ltd., 1961. 11–28.

Bauer, Dale M. *Feminist Dialogics: A Theory of Failed Community*. Albany: State University of New York Press, 1988.

Baym, Nina. *Woman's Fiction: A Guide to Novels by and about Women in America, 1820–1870*. Ithaca: Cornell University Press, 1978.

Beauvoir, Simone de. *The Second Sex*. Translated and edited by H. M. Parshley. New York: Bantam, 1974.

Bell, Millicent. *Edith Wharton & Henry James: The Story of Their Friendship*. New York: George Braziller, 1965.

Bem, Sandra L., and Daryl J. Bem. "Case Study of a Nonconscious Ideology: Training the Woman to Know Her Place." *Beliefs, Attitudes, and Human Affairs*. By Daryl Bem. Belmont, California: Brooks/Cole Publishing Company, 1970. 89–99.

Bewley, Marius. "Mrs. Wharton's Mask." *Masks & Mirrors: Essays in Criticism*. New York: Atheneum, 1970. 145–153.

Bonner, Thomas, Jr. *The Kate Chopin Companion: With Chopin's Translations from French Fiction*. New York: Greenwood Press, 1988.

Brenni, Vito J. *Edith Wharton: A Bibliography*. Morgantown: West Virginia University Library, 1966.

Bristol, Marie. "Life Among the Ungentle Genteel: Edith Wharton's

The House of Mirth Revisited." *Western Humanities Review* 16 (Autumn 1962): 371–374.

Brown, E. K. *Edith Wharton: Etude critique.* Paris: E. Droz, 1935.

Collins, Joseph. *Taking the Literary Pulse: Psychological Studies of Life and Letters.* New York: George H. Doran Company, 1924.

Coontz, Stephanie. *The Social Origins of Private Life: A History of American Families 1600–1900.* London: Verso, 1988.

Cott, Nancy F. *The Bonds of Womanhood: 'Woman's Sphere' in New England, 1780–1835.* New Haven: Yale University Press, 1977.

———, ed. *Root of Bitterness: Documents of the Social History of American Women.* New York: E. P. Dutton & Co., Inc., 1972.

Crowley, John W. "The Unmastered Streak: Feminist Themes in Wharton's *Summer.*" *American Literary Realism, 1870–1910* 15.1 (Spring 1982): 86–96.

Culley, Margaret. ed. The Awakening: *An Authoritative Text, Contexts, Criticism.* New York: W. W. Norton & Company, Inc., 1976.

Degler, Carl N. *At Odds: Women and the Family in America from the Revolution to the Present.* New York: Oxford University Press, 1980.

Dimock, Wai-chee. "Debasing Exchange: Edith Wharton's *The House of Mirth.*" *PMLA* 100.5 (October 1985): 783–792.

Donovan, Josephine. *After the Fall: The Demeter-Persephone Myth in Wharton, Cather, and Glasgow.* University Park: Pennsylvania State University Press, 1989.

Drew, Elizabeth A. "Is There a 'Feminine' Fiction?" *The Modern Novel: Some Aspects of Contemporary Fiction.* New York: Harcourt, Brace and Company, 1926. 101–116.

The Edith Wharton Newsletter. Edited by Annette Zilversmit, Long Island University. 1984—.

Elfenbein, Anna Shannon. *Women on the Color Line: Evolving Stereotypes and the Writings of George Washington Cable, Grace King, Kate Chopin.* Charlottesville: University Press of Virginia, 1989.

Emerson, Ralph Waldo. "Woman." *Miscellanies.* Boston: Houghton Mifflin Company, 1878. 403–426.

Ewell, Barbara C. *Kate Chopin.* New York: Ungar Publishing Co., 1986.

Fetterley, Judith. *The Resisting Reader: A Feminist Approach to American Fiction.* Bloomington: Indiana University Press, 1978.

———. " 'The Temptation to be a Beautiful Object': Double Standard and Double Bind in *The House of Mirth.*" *Studies in American Fiction* 5.2 (Autumn 1977): 199–211.

Flanner, Janet (Genêt). "Edith Wharton (1862–1937)." *Paris was Yesterday (1925–1939).* Edited by Irving Drutman. New York: Popular Library, 1972. 171–178.

Foucault, Michel. *The Archaeology of Knowledge & The Discourse on Language*. Translated by A. M. Sheridan Smith. New York: Harper & Row, Publishers, 1972.

Franklin, Rosemary F. "*The Awakening* and the Failure of Pysche." *American Literature* 56.4 (December 1984): 510–516.

Friedan, Betty. *The Feminine Mystique*. New York: Dell, 1975.

Friedman, Lawrence J. *Inventors of the Promised Land*. New York: Alfred A. Knopf, 1975.

Fryer, Judith. *Felicitous Space: The Imaginative Structures of Edith Wharton and Willa Cather*. Chapel Hill: University of North Carolina Press, 1986.

Gilman, Charlotte Perkins. *The Home: Its Work and Influence*. Urbana: University of Illinois Press, 1972.

―――. *The Man-Made World or, Our Androcentric Culture*. New York: Charlton Company, 1911.

―――. *Women & Economics: A Study of the Economic Relation Between Men and Women as a Factor in Social Evolution*. Edited by Carl Degler. New York: Harper & Row, 1966.

Gimbel, Wendy. *Edith Wharton: Orphancy and Survival*. New York: Praeger Publishers, 1984.

Goode, John. "Woman and the Literary Text." *The Rights and Wrongs of Women*. Edited by Juliet Mitchell and Ann Oakley. New York: Penguin Books, Ltd., 1976. 217–255.

Gordon, Ann D., Mari Jo Buhle, and Nancy E. Schrom. *Women in American Society*. Cambridge, Massachusetts: Radical America, 1972.

Hackett, Francis. *Horizons: A Book of Criticisms*. New York: B. W. Huebsch, 1918.

Hardy, Thomas. *Jude the Obscure*. London: Macmillan & Co., Ltd., 1920.

―――. *Tess of the D'Urbervilles: A Pure Woman*. London: Macmillan & Co., Ltd., 1920.

Harris, Barbara J. *Beyond Her Sphere: Women and the Professions in American History*. Westport: Greenwood Press, 1978.

Harvey, John. "Contrasting Worlds: A Study in the Novels of Edith Wharton." *Etudes anglaises* 7 (April 1954): 190–198.

Hazard, Caroline. *Some Ideals in the Education of Women*. New York: Thomas Y. Crowell & Co., Publishers, 1900.

Hicks, Granville. *The Great Tradition: An Interpretation of American Literature Since the Civil War*. Revised edition. New York: Biblo and Tannen, 1935 and 1967.

Huf, Linda. *A Portrait of the Artist as a Young Woman: The Writer as Heroine in American Literature*. New York: Frederick Ungar, 1983.

Irigaray, Luce. *Speculum of the Other Woman.* Translated by Gillian C. Gill. Ithaca: Cornell University Press, 1985.

———. *This Sex Which is Not One.* Translated by Catherine Porter. Ithaca: Cornell University Press, 1985.

Jacobus, Mary, ed. *Women Writing and Writing about Women.* New York: Barnes & Noble Books, 1979.

James, Henry. *The Letters of Henry James.* 2 volumes. Selected and edited by Percy Lubbock. London: Macmillan and Co., Limited, 1920.

———. "The New Novel: 1914." *Notes on Novelists; with Some Other Notes.* New York: Charles Scribner's Sons, 1914. 314–361.

Jameson, Fredric. *The Political Unconscious: Narrative as a Socially Symbolic Act.* Ithaca: Cornell University Press, 1981.

Jones, Anne Goodwyn. *Tomorrow Is Another Day: The Woman Writer in the South, 1859–1936.* Baton Rouge: Louisiana State University Press, 1981.

Joslin, Katherine. "Edith Wharton at 125." *College Literature* 14.3 (Fall 1987): 193–206.

Kaplan, Amy. *The Social Construction of American Realism.* Chicago: University of Chicago Press, 1988.

The Kate Chopin Newsletter. Edited by Emily Toth. Volumes I-II (Spring 1975-Winter 1976–1977); *Regionalism and the Female Imagination.* Volumes III-IV (Spring 1977-Winter 1979).

Kelley, Mary, ed. *Woman's Being, Woman's Place: Female Identity and Vocation in American History.* Boston: G. K. Hall & Co., 1979.

Kellogg (Griffith), Grace. *The Two Lives of Edith Wharton: The Woman and Her Work.* New York: Appleton-Century, 1965.

Klinkowitz, Jerome. "Kate Chopin's Awakening to Naturalism." *The Practice of Fiction in America· Writers from Hawthorne to the Present.* Ames: Iowa State University Press, 1980. 38–48.

Koloski, Bernard, ed. *Approaches to Teaching Chopin's* The Awakening. Approaches to Teaching World Literature 16. New York: MLA, 1988.

Kronenberger, Louis. "Edith Wharton: *The Age of Innocence* and *The House of Mirth.*" *The Polished Surface: Essays in the Literature of Worldliness.* New York: Alfred A. Knopf, 1969. 246–270.

Ladenson, Joyce Ruddel. "The Return of St. Louis' Prodigal Daughter: Kate Chopin after Seventy Years." *Midamerica: The Yearbook of the Society for the Study of Midwestern Literature.* Edited by David D. Anderson. East Lansing: Midwestern Press (Michigan State University), 1975. II, 24–34.

Lattin, Patricia Hopkins. "Childbirth and Motherhood in Kate Chopin's Fiction." *Regionalism and the Female Imagination* 4.1 (Spring 1978): 8–12.

Leary, Lewis. *Southern Excursions. Essays on Mark Twain and Others.* Baton Rouge: Louisiana State University Press, 1971.

Lee, Brian. *American Fiction, 1865–1940.* London: Longman, 1987.

Lewis, R.W.B. *Edith Wharton: A Biography.* New York: Harper & Row, 1977.

Lubbock, Percy. *Portrait of Edith Wharton.* New York: Appleton-Century-Crofts and London: Jonathan Cape, 1947.

Lyde, Marilyn Jones. *Edith Wharton: Convention and Morality in the Work of a Novelist.* Norman: University of Oklahoma Press, 1959.

McDowell, Margaret B. *Edith Wharton.* Boston: Twayne Publishers, 1976.

Martin, Wendy, ed. *New Essays on* The Awakening. Cambridge: Cambridge University Press, 1988.

Martineau, Harriet. *Society in America.* 2 volumes. New York: Saunders & Otley, 1837.

Millgate, Michael. "Edith Wharton." *American Social Fiction: James to Cozzens.* London: Oliver & Boyd, 1964. 54–66.

Minh-ha, Trinh T. *Woman, Native, Other: Writing Postcoloniality and Feminism.* Bloomington: Indiana University Press, 1989.

Montgomery, Judith H. "The American Galatea." *College English* 32 (May 1971): 890–899.

Morris, Lloyd. *Postscript to Yesterday: American Life and Thought, 1896–1946.* New York: Harper & Row, 1947 and 1965.

Nevius, Blake. *Edith Wharton: A Study of Her Fiction.* Berkeley: University of California Press, 1953 and 1961.

Newman, Louise Michele, ed. *Men's Ideas/Women's Realities:* Popular Science, *1870–1915.* New York: Pergamon Press, 1985.

Nightingale, Florence. *Cassandra.* Introduction by Myra Stark. Epilogue by Cynthia Macdonald. Old Westbury, NY: The Feminist Press, 1979.

Papashvily, Helen Waite. *All the Happy Endings: A Study of the Domestic Novel in America, the Women Who Wrote It, the Women Who Read It, in the Nineteenth-Century.* New York: Harper & Brothers Publishers, 1956.

Parr, Susan Resneck. *The Moral of the Story: Literature, Values, and American Education.* New York: Teachers College Press, 1982.

Parrington, Vernon L. *The Beginnings of Critical Realism in America, 1860–1920.* Volume Three of *Main Currents in American Thought.* New York: Harcourt, Brace & World, Inc., 1930 and 1958.

Plante, Patricia R. "Edith Wharton: A Prophet Without Due Honor." *Midwest Review* (1962): 16–22.

Rankin, Daniel S. *Kate Chopin and Her Creole Stories.* Philadelphia: University of Pennsylvania Press, 1932.

Rich, Adrienne. "Literary Concepts of 'The Universal' is False Notion." *College English* 43.2 (February 1981): 191–192.

Roller, Judi M. *The Politics of the Feminist Novel.* Westport, CT: Greenwood Press, 1986.

Rothman, Sheila M. *Woman's Proper Place: A History of Changing Ideals and Practices, 1870 to the Present.* New York: Basic Books Inc., 1978.

Scott, Anne Firor. "Women's Perspective on the Patriarchy in the 1850's." *Journal of American History* 61.1 (June 1974): 52–64.

Seyersted, Per. *Kate Chopin: A Critical Biography.* Baton Rouge: Louisiana State University Press, 1969 and 1980.

Skaggs, Peggy. *Kate Chopin.* Boston: Twayne, 1985.

Smith-Rosenberg, Carroll. *Disorderly Conduct: Visions of Gender in Victorian America.* New York: Oxford University Press, 1986.

Sontag, Susan. "The Pornographic Imagination." *Styles of Radical Will.* New York: Dell Publishing Co., Inc., 1969. 35–73.

Taylor, Helen. *Gender, Race, and Region in the Writings of Grace King, Ruth McEnery Stuart, and Kate Chopin.* Baton Rouge: Louisiana State University Press, 1989.

Toth, Emily. "The Cult of Domesticity and 'A Sentimental Soul.' " *Kate Chopin Newsletter* 1.2 (Fall 1975): 9–16.

———. "The Independent Woman and 'Free' Love." *Massachusetts Review* 16 (Autumn 1975): 647–664.

———. "Kate Chopin and Literary Convention: 'Désirée's Baby.' " *Southern Studies* 20 (Summer 1981): 201–208.

———. "Kate Chopin's *The Awakening* as Feminist Criticism." *Louisiana Studies* 15.3 (Fall 1976): 241–251.

———. "St. Louis and the Fiction of Kate Chopin." *Missouri Historical Society Bulletin* 32 (October 1975): 33–50.

———. "That Outward Existence Which Conforms: Kate Chopin and Literary Convention." Diss. Johns Hopkins University, 1975.

———. "Timely and Timeless: The Treatment of Time in *The Awakening* and *Sister Carrie*." *Southern Studies* 16 (Fall 1977): 271–276.

Turner, Jean. "The Ideology of Women in the Fiction of Edith Wharton 1899–1920." Diss. University of Wisconsin-Madison, 1975.

Tutwiler, Julia R. "Edith Wharton in New York City." *Women Authors of Our Day in Their Homes: Personal Descriptions and Interviews.* Edited by Francis W. Halsey. New York: James Pott & Company, 1903. 241–247.

Tyler, Ralph. "Edith Wharton." *Bookviews* 1.12 (August 1978): 26–27.

Underwood, John Curtis. "Culture and Edith Wharton." *Literature and Insurgency: Ten Studies in Racial Evolution.* New York: Biblo & Tannen, 1914 and 1974. 346–390.

Valdivia, Olga Avendaño de. "Edith Wharton. Mrs. Wharton's Philosophy of Life—Her Conception of Morality. Minor Moral Problems." *Andean Quarterly* (Winter 1944): 56–72.

Veblen, Thorstein. *Essays in Our Changing Order*. Edited by Leon
Ardzrooni. New York: Viking Press, 1934.

———. *The Theory of the Leisure Class: An Economic Study of Institutions*.
New York: Modern Library, 1934.

Vidal, Gore. Introduction. *The Edith Wharton Omnibus*. By Edith Wharton. New York: Nelson Doubleday, Inc., 1978. vii–xiii.

Walton, Geoffrey. *Edith Wharton: A Critical Interpretation*. Second revised
edition. Rutherford: Fairleigh Dickinson University Press, 1982.

Welter, Barbara. *Dimity Convictions: The American Woman in the Nineteenth
Century*. Athens: Ohio University Press, 1976.

Williams, Raymond. *Marxism and Literature*. Oxford: Oxford University
Press, 1977.

Wilson, Edmund. "Justice to Edith Wharton." *The Wound and the Bow:
Seven Studies in Literature*. Cambridge: Riverside Press, 1941. 195–
213.

Wolf, Christa. *The Quest for Christa T.* Translated by Christopher Mid-
dleton. New York: Farrar, Straus and Giroux, Inc., 1970.

Wolff, Cynthia Griffin. *A Feast of Words: The Triumph of Edith Wharton*.
New York: Oxford University Press, 1977.

———. "Kate Chopin and the Fiction of Limits: 'Désirée's Baby.' " *Southern Literary Journal* 10.2 (1978): 123–133.

Woolf, Virginia. *Women and Writing*. Edited and with an Introduction
by Michèle Barrett. New York: Harcourt Brace Jovanovich, 1979.

Index

About the Author

MARY E. PAPKE is an Assistant Professor of English at the University of Tennessee, Knoxville. She is also an assistant editor of *Literature and Psychology*. Papke has contributed articles and essays to *Approaches to Teaching Chopin's* The Awakening, *Literature and Psychology, Tulsa Studies in Women's Literature, Telos,* and *The Sean O'Casey Review.*